HARLEM☀MOON
BROADWAY

Harlem Moon
Broadway Books
New York

Saving the Race

CONVERSATIONS ABOUT DU BOIS FROM

A Collective Memoir of Souls

REBECCA CARROLL

Published by Harlem Moon,
an imprint of Broadway Books,
a division of Random House, Inc.

PRINTED IN THE UNITED STATES OF AMERICA

HARLEM MOON, BROADWAY BOOKS, and the HARLEM MOON
logo, depicting a moon and a woman, are trademarks of Random
House, Inc. The figure in the Harlem Moon logo is inspired by a
graphic design by Aaron Douglas (1899–1979).

Visit our website at www.harlemmoon.com

First edition published July 2004

Library of Congress Cataloging-in-Publication Data
Carroll, Rebecca.
Saving the race : conversations about Du Bois from a collective
memoir of souls / Rebecca Carroll.—1st ed.
p.   cm.
1. Du Bois, W. E. B. (William Edward Burghardt), 1868–1963. Souls of
Black folk. 2. Du Bois, W. E. B. (William Edward Burghardt),
1868–1963—Political and social views. 3. Du Bois, W. E. B. (William
Edward Burghardt), 1868–1963—Influence. 4. African
Americans—Interviews. 5. African Americans—Social conditions. 6.
African Americans—Race identity. I. Title.
E185.6.D797325 2004
920'.009296073—dc22
2003067777

ISBN 0-7679-1619-0

10   9   8   7   6   5   4   3   2   1

WILDERMUTH

For Monique, Beck, and Larc

I PRAY YOU, THEN, RECEIVE MY LITTLE BOOK IN ALL CHARITY, STUDYING MY WORDS WITH ME, FORGIVING MISTAKE AND FOIBLE FOR SAKE OF THE FAITH AND PASSION THAT IS IN ME, AND SEEKING THE GRAIN OF TRUTH HIDDEN THERE.

—W. E. B. Du Bois,
The Souls of Black Folk

Contents

Acknowledgments

I wish to first extend deep thanks for continued support and encouragement from my family—especially my parents, David and Laurette Carroll; also Renny Waldron, Laura Perkins, Sean Carroll, Riana Frost, Jennifer Berkeley, Gary Waldron, Pepe Lopez, and Kiko Lopez. And to the following friends, writers, readers, honest critics, and genuine champions: Sherman Alexie, Peter Glenshaw, Annie Burke, Tim Dansdill, Christy Cox, Agnes Burke, Patricia Gaines, Randy Dottin, and Derek Loosvelt.

ACKNOWLEDGMENTS

I would like to express my gratitude for the monthlong writing residency I was awarded at the Jentel Artist Residency Program in Banner, Wyoming, which allowed me to write the first draft of this book. I am grateful to Sandy Scott and Judy Sutcliffe, and all the fine people of Galena, Illinois, where I was lucky enough to spend two quiet and simple months working on the second draft of this book. I am appreciative for the generosity extended to me by A Room of Her Own Foundation in Placitas, New Mexico. I am heartened by the fact that my keen and unassailable agent, Meredith Bernstein, keeps believing in me and selling my work. And finally, I am delighted to have had the opportunity to work with my editor on this book, Janet Hill, whose feedback and insights were integral to my finishing these pages.

Saving the Race

Prologue

I started this book with the sense that I could introduce new language and produce original content based on and inspired by themes set forth in the 1903 classic essay collection, *The Souls of Black Folk*, by W. E. B. Du Bois. I wanted to know how contemporary black Americans maintain, uphold, and reconcile (or not) with the words and prophesies Du Bois expressed in *Souls*, and I wanted to explore thoughts within and beyond the more immediately recognizable concepts in the book: "One ever feels his two-ness—an American, a Negro; two souls, two thoughts, two unreconciled strivings; two warring ideals in one dark body, whose dogged strength alone keeps it from being torn asunder." What *of* the dogged strength? Is it not, in part, the experience and rawness from being torn asunder that makes black culture what it is?

There are many extraordinary theses presented in *The Souls of Black Folk*, the body of which has been studied, critiqued, and analyzed primarily through academic channels over the past century. Indeed, last year marked the centennial of the book's publication, celebrated by any number of conferences, lectures, on-line Web casts, and other noteworthy presentations. I thought, however, that it would also be important to pair the ideas in *Souls* with individuals not just from academe but from black culture at large. Individuals who may represent the choice to stay six degrees of closeness to the pain of slave history and who have built careers and perhaps created demagogies around that choice. Many have cultivated what feels to them like irreparable psychological hurt and emotional damage. Maybe it is irreparable. And maybe it is not. Maybe it is entirely reparable. If black Americans are given a choice about whether or not to stay connected to, pained and damaged by, slave history, is the choice always yes? And, of course, more important, does the choice exist, or will it ever? Many black Americans would question the authenticity of this author's blackness based on such questioning alone.

"The problem of the twentieth century is the problem of the color-line," Du Bois wrote, memorably, in *Souls*. And still, too, the problem of the twenty-first century. The writing of this book is cogent for me not only because of the insights I hope it may reveal about ways in which the problem of the color line continues to shape black America but also because of my desire to settle the problem of my own more personal, privatized color line.

I am biracial—a white birth mother and a black birth father—and I was adopted and raised by white parents. The ambiguity surrounding my racial identity as a young girl prompted the somewhat unsettling phrase "culturally white and cosmetically black," which I heard for the first time from my birth mother, whom I will call Tess, and with whom I reunited when I was eleven years old. I feel, though, that I am more like what Du Bois termed in his *Souls* essay "Of the Training of Black Men," a "tertium quid." Not, perhaps, as he wrote, like "a clownish, simple creature," but certainly "at times even lovable within its limitations, but straightly foreordained to walk within the Veil."

Brown-skinned in variations of light to semilight but not often dark, articulate English-non-Ebonics-speaking, not terribly down but willing to be identified as or associated with folks who are, asked to choose sides if push comes to shove, demanded upon to prove authenticity at practically every streetlight, street fight, throw-down, SAT boycott, student union meeting, political rally, hair salon, and first date—I am among the first generation for whom this particular identity is socially prevalent: the biracial entity. In turns, a step above the tragic mulatto, and a generation or two removed from the master and his slave mistress; the child made of curious white girls and angry black boys, or less often angry black girls and curious white boys, seduced by the rage and revolution of the sixties—the child then heroically kept or stoically given away, ever still a product of charged, semiprivileged rebellion and abandonment, sure to bring about a new race and species of understanding. Does my soul matter?

As best as I can recall, it was Tess who introduced me to *The Souls of Black Folk*. Although my adopted parents had made me aware of my blackness as best they could, they did not seek out ways and means to define it for me. Tess did. This included her giving me Maya Angelou's *I Know Why the Caged Bird Sings* for our first Christmas together, and a legion of verbal embassages on black cultural behavior based solely on her own general expertise.

Later on, I learned that when Tess was growing up, her mother—a dark, afflicted, and self-invented aristocratic Anglophile with a legendary intellect, well cultivated and preserved by her proud, if abandoned, progeny—had often held salons, which included many black writers and artists, in the living room of their home in Boston's Hyde Park. I discovered, too, that Tess's white jazz pianist father had played in what was then widely considered to be Boston's first integrated jazz band. But at this time—my being preadolescent at best and having encountered maybe all of three black people in my life at that point—I certainly was not intent on, or even thinking about, checking Tess's credentials on the matter of black culture.

There was, though, a copy of *Souls* in the dusty, over-crowded bookshelves of the late-eighteenth-century Colonial house where I grew up in rural New Hampshire, before I began spending large amounts of time with Tess at her apartment on the New England seacoast about sixty-five miles east. It was probably even close to a first edition, but for whatever reasons, I was never drawn to it, even though its spine sat emboldened between other books I liked—*The Boxcar Children*, *Wagtail*, and *The Lion, the Witch and the Wardrobe*. And, since I didn't learn much in the way of black literature at the small regional high school I attended, I didn't come upon *Souls* in any kind of meaningful way until it held an association to Tess and what she was trying to teach me in order for me to become a better person—not necessarily a better black person, but at least a better white person with a knowledge of black people.

She didn't give me the book outright; rather, she imposed its significance upon me, as she did the significance of many things, as most parents (birth or otherwise) are wont to do. But in this case, she was principally concerned with the significance of things pertaining to black culture and literature. Subsequently, I didn't actually read the book, but, rather, acquired a sense of its importance, an awareness I then took with me to college, where I encountered my first black professor. Reading *Souls* for the first time, particularly under the tutelage of an older, handsome, and astute black man with my best interests at heart, was a humbling experience, and also something like stopping at the top of a Ferris wheel and then swinging the bucket seat—dangerous, exciting, while ultimately, and essentially, liberating.

Naturally, the idea for this book was further impelled by my own relationship to the construct of race, along with its very specific yet bewildering appeal to me. Up until a few years ago, writing and interviewing had been for me the surest outlet for considering the complexities surrounding race. Through narrative interviews with black people in America (first contemporary writers, then teenage girls), I was able to ask questions, draw the occasional parallel, and hear stories that I desperately needed to hear and would not have otherwise heard. But by the end of my third book, I felt tired and worn out from what seemed, finally, like an attempt to appropriate black culture.

I took some time off from writing. First, I worked as a producer for *The Charlie Rose Show* on PBS, and then I worked at two separate dot-com start-ups. At all three jobs, I felt the pressure to represent, the desire to represent, and the resentment about having to represent my blackness. I remember getting into an argument with one of my colleagues at *Charlie Rose* over who *should* produce the black guests. "I don't see why you should produce the black guests just because you're black," he said to me, when I was about five months into the job and had raised the issue on my own. "I've built a relationship with these people," he continued.

Now, I'm fairly certain that he didn't mean "these people" in *that* way, but I didn't really care. I was fed up and frustrated with the politically correct requirements and protocol of properly "representing" and, also, about feeling as though I'd been hired for this particular job, in part, because up until then there had been no black perspective on the show. If I'm going to be that perspective, then I damn well better get to produce a segment with Laurence Fishburne, I thought.

At Africana.com—"Gateway to the Black World"—I was immersed all day, every day, with news and information having to do exclusively with black people and culture. I confess to being slightly stunned by, if admittedly naïve about, how separate and segregated our country still is: black news, black television shows, black magazines, black search engines, all in the face of the "dominant culture." When I told white people what dot com I worked for, even though it was the brainchild of Henry Louis Gates, Jr., one of the country's best-known academics and essayists, most had never heard of it.

Next, at Contentville.com, a literary, content-driven Web site launched by media mogul Steve Brill, I again felt that familiar jumble of emotions concerning my cultural positioning and the expectations behind it, and I knew that it would be this way forever unless I changed it for myself. This is to say, it would always be an issue of allegiance regarding a choice between *Essence* or *Elle*, *Charlie Rose* or *Tavis Smiley*, Africana.com or Contentville.com.

Enough, I thought.

It occurred to me that perhaps the best source to help create a resolve would be *The Souls of Black Folk*. I read and reread *Souls*, marking and pasting Post-it notes where passages struck me, shook me; then I paired these passages with leading black voices in America that I felt were offering or had offered some of the most vividly affecting commentary in recent time, and, too, who were living out, in effect, what Du Bois predicted in *Souls*. I next prefaced these passages with evolutionary glimpses into my own black consciousness. This, then, is not a scholarly offering, nor an academic analysis of *The Souls of Black Folk*; rather, it is a collective memoir of souls . . . the souls of black folk.

What follows is a collection of interviews in narrative form, woven together by the thread of personal memoir; each chapter begins with a quote from *The Souls of Black Folk*, evocative of the book itself, which features a "bar of the Sorrow Songs,—some echo of haunting melody from the only American music which welled up from black souls in the dark past." In this context, Du Bois's visionary observations are, too, bars of a haunting melody, yet they are welled up from only one black soul with the hope of leading us all to a brighter future.

When I was writing this book—piecing passages together, transcribing interviews, rereading *The Souls of Black Folk*—and people would ask me what it was about, I would start by saying that it was part memoir and part social commentary on race in America, using a literary classic as reference and semi-model. It's a mouthful. And I would almost always get the same expression in response: "Huh?"

Most writers know that you may start with one idea for a book or an article, or whatever it may be, and often the idea will have evolved into something entirely different by the time you near the end. This book is no exception. I wanted first and foremost to honor and reintroduce W. E. B. Du Bois and *The Souls of Black Folk* in a way that is accessible and through a genre I am comfortable with and that has been effective in the past as a tool to communicate the various issues germane to race in America—oral history as narrative nonfiction.

As I began selecting interview subjects for the book, I

knew that I would want to explain at least somewhat before the start of each narrative why I had chosen that particular person. I did not intend for the explanations to become short memoir pieces, but with each Du Bois quote an experience of mine virtually insinuated itself to the page. The memories rushed and escaped and demanded page time. And that is precisely when I realized my life had always existed behind the Veil and that I now needed both to stay there and to show a way into this strange, surreal place where we of darker skin live, just as Du Bois had done in order to write *The Souls of Black Folk*: "Leaving, then, the world of the white man, I have stepped within the Veil, raising it that you may view faintly its deeper recesses. . . ."

The interviews, then, are voices from behind the Veil, offering insight into "the meaning of [the Veil's] religion, the passion of its human sorrow, and the struggle of its greater souls." But they are also shifting voices, self-invented voices, irreverent and elegant voices—voices that go beyond the religion, human sorrow, and struggle of the Veiled life. They are voices we can learn from and that "if read with patience may show the strange meaning of being black here in the dawning" of the twenty-first century.

My intention in using the medium of narrative interviews is to offer a seamless blend of social commentary, literary journalism, and individual voice. The interviews here are not verbatim transcripts; they are reshaped and in many instances rewritten, with additional input from interview subjects, by this author (except in the case of Derrick Bell, who largely rewrote his own narrative).

The interview subjects are: novelist and Oprah Book Club author Lalita Tademy; cultural critic and novelist Stanley Crouch; Madam C. J. Walker's biographer and great-great-granddaughter, A'Lelia Bundles; the stepson of W. E. B. Du Bois, David Graham Du Bois; novelist, essayist, and *Rolling Stone* contributor Touré; NAACP chairman Julian Bond; the deputy director of exhibitions at the Studio Museum of Harlem, Thelma Golden; managing director of Lazard Freres & Co., former president and CEO of the National Urban League, Inc., and former executive director of the United Negro College Fund, Vernon E. Jordan, Jr.; former communications secretary of the Black Panther party, civil rights activist, and memoirist Kathleen Cleaver; former New Jersey councilman and community activist Cory Booker; founder and president of the National Coalition of 100 Black Women, Jewell Jackson McCabe; New York University Law School professor Derrick Bell; senior minister of Riverside Church in New York, the Reverend James Forbes; poet Patricia Smith; film composer Terence Blanchard; poet, essayist, and playwright Elizabeth Alexander; writer, painter, and poet Clarence Major; and LeAlan Jones, coauthor with Lloyd Newman of *Our America: Life and Death on the Southside of Chicago*.

Please note that, out of respect for their privacy, I have changed the names of many of the people who appear in this book.

REBECCA CARROLL, 2004

Chapter One

NO GENERATION REMOVED

> . . . NO PEOPLE A GENERATION REMOVED FROM SLAVERY
> CAN ESCAPE A CERTAIN UNPLEASANT RAWNESS AND
> GAUCHERIE, DESPITE THE BEST OF TRAINING.
>
> —"Of the Training of Black Men"

On a brisk autumn day in 1978, my best friend and I ran around the playground during recess, joyfully winded, pushing and pulling, giggling out loud. The fifth-grade class in our small-town elementary school was split into two sections, taught by two different teachers: Mrs. Emerson, known as "the nice one," and Mrs. James, known as "the mean one." My best friend almost since birth, Leah, had Mrs. Emerson, and I had Mrs. James. Recess was the one time that Leah and I were able to play together, and we waited for the twenty-minute break each day for that reason alone.

On this particular day, Mrs. James was the teacher on recess duty. I never thought she was all that bad. I was a good student, engaged and outgoing. As far as I could tell, I was in decent standing with Mrs. James. She could lose her temper, but she'd never lost it at me. After a straight, plain, satisfying game of tag, Leah and I dashed up to the dirt mound that served as a watch point overlooking the playground, where Mrs. James stood. Maybe we wanted to say hello, or to win brownie points. I don't remember. Mrs. James, with her thick hands crammed inside a fur muff and a weighty wool coat buttoned up to her chin as small puffs of visible breath drifted from her broad frame, studied us fixedly.

"You're a very pretty girl, Leah," she said. Indeed a pretty girl, Leah grinned, pleased, her cheeks rosy and taut, her teeth chattering slightly. "And you're very pretty, too, Becky," she said, imparting a clear, frank glance, "for a black girl."

It wasn't the content of what Mrs. James said, as I had no earthly idea what being "pretty, for a black girl" meant. It was her tone, the implication of which very abruptly set out clear and present boundaries as to what was okay to be and what was not okay to be. I was fully aware of having brown skin, but I had never felt inferior because of it. This was the first time in my life that I realized it would close doors to me. Not only close doors but slam them. It felt horrible, and so completely, instinctively wrong. Sure, it was wrong to talk during class, but this, this strange, loaded, and seemingly uniform remark, felt *wrong*.

In the opening essay of *The Souls of Black Folk*, "Of Our Spiritual Strivings," Du Bois writes of an experience similar in its swift and utter decimation of youthful spirit. In the "wee wooden schoolhouse" that he attended as a child, one who, coincidentally, also grew up in New England, the schoolchildren decide to buy and exchange greeting cards as a way of getting to know one another. "The exchange was merry," Du Bois recalls, until one of the girls refused to accept his card—"refused it peremptorily." It was then that Du Bois realized "with a certain suddenness" that he was different from the other children, and would then forever be "shut out from their world by a vast veil."

In the statement that opens this essay—"no people a generation removed from slavery can escape a certain unpleasantness and gaucherie, despite the best of training"—Du Bois is making specific reference to the odds of lasting success and mainstream assimilation for "Negro college-bred men" in the early 1900s, indicating a kind of self-awareness among them that allowed for an understanding of their limitations, given the context in which they were trying to achieve any success at all. But I thought of the quote more in terms of how slavery has produced this inescapable strain that courses through the veins of every subsequent generation of people—black, white, and other—in varying degrees.

Du Bois's experience and mine demonstrate the remarkable and unsettling ease with which people sometimes express a prejudice that they perhaps did not even cultivate on their own—one that came with them as part of the package they were born with, like a random blood cell or a useless calcium deposit. That said, however, the prejudice Du Bois experienced circa 1875 is less than he would have experienced in 1865, and the prejudice I experienced in 1978 is less than I would have experienced in 1968.

The novel *Cane River* by Lalita Tademy, based in part on the author's own family history, follows the lives of four black women on the Louisiana River during the late 1800s and early 1900s. The saga begins with Suzette, a thirteen-year-old light-skinned house slave, who is raped by the relative of her master, which then leads to her becoming his mistress and having two children by him. One of her children, a daughter named Philomene, even more light-skinned than her mother, also becomes the mistress of a white man, and so on. Both during and after the abolishment of slavery, each woman continues the pattern of having children with white men, thereby diluting the brownness of their skin, although never the strength of their identities as black American women.

As the plot of Lalita Tademy's novel speaks to the enduring impact of slavery, so too, conversely, does the fact that the novel was chosen as an Oprah Book Club selection in 2001. Oprah Winfrey, both the person and the entity, is arguably as far removed from the vestiges of slavery as anyone in America can get. While her endorsement of *Cane River* brought attention to the cultural history that bore her and many others, because of her great crossover success and fortune—save her brilliant turn as Sofia in Steven Spielberg's film adaptation of Alice Walker's novel *The Color Purple* and, later, her notable efforts in making the movie version of Toni Morrison's novel

Beloved, the story of an ex-slave who cannot escape the demons of her past—it is a cultural history with which Winfrey is seldom immediately associated.

My playground, Du Bois's rejected greeting card, and the novel *Cane River*, while disparate examples in many ways, come together to create a narrative that conveys the shared pain, humiliation, shame, and peculiar evolution of suffering experienced by successive generations removed from slavery.

Lalita Tademy

I would say that no *people* removed from slavery are able to escape. Not just one generation removed. *All* people who have slavery in their conscious background cannot escape, which is exactly what I saw happening with the women in *Cane River*, the women in my own personal history.

One of the things that I did not want to do with *Cane River* was to write it in such a way that the brutality of slavery could be attributed to physical pain. The heartbreak for the women in this story, which also happens to be true, is not due to beating; it's due to separation—the things that happen to their family, the invasion of their personal selves, and the threat to their children. It's due to not being allowed to form relationships. I didn't want to get lost in the story of coming over from Africa in the hulls of boats, or in what is very well documented everywhere—the physical whippings and beatings and subjugation of slavery. I wanted to show subjugation of the soul.

I have had people challenge me on the characters in the book, and the fact that they are slaves and yet did not get beaten. But far more people have said that they were drawn in by these women and felt a need to understand what happened to them, how they evolved and made a life for themselves. Many people say they had no idea that this sort of constant threat existed at that time—that members of slave families were always a moment away from being separated from one another.

One of the reasons that I wrote *Cane River*, and why I wrote it the way I did, was because I knew my grandfather, who appears as Emily's son T.O. in the book. And although T.O. looked very white, so much so that he could easily have passed, he never, ever, would have been able to pass in his own mind. Toward the end of the book, after he's gone through such psychological trauma, he decides that the best thing he could do to honor his family's legacy is to marry a darker-skinned black woman. Here was a man who was, by physical appearance, no longer constrained, but mentally the boundaries were still there. He couldn't have escaped the constraint if he'd wanted to. It was not in his being.

I think the inability or ability to escape slave history for black Americans has certainly evolved since the time that I was writing about—the story in *Cane River* begins in 1834 and ends in 1936—and that, as our options expand, there is more room to explore and struggle in different ways. Traveling around to promote the book and deliver lectures, I've had a considerable number of mixed-race people flock to me to tell me about their individual choices; they talk about their ability to choose who they want to be, which is so very different from being as rigidly defined as black people were a hundred or so years ago, when some felt the need to slip out of their skin in order to have choices. You might have been able to do it by how you looked, but you also had to do it emotionally. And today, that just isn't the case. We're talking about a bell curve, where there are two different tails and people can gravitate to one tail or the other. What I'm saying is that the bell curve is broader than it used to be, and able to accommodate many more diverse behaviors and reactions.

When I was growing up, I knew I had white blood in me, but I actually didn't give it much thought, because my personal upbringing was definitively black. There was no wavering on that, even though my mother looked white, which only meant that when we moved in somewhere, she went to sign the rental papers. Or, if we were driving through the South, she would be the one to do the driving, and the rest of us would duck down in our seats. That was just logistics. It was for practical purposes. She never went to bed white, even if sometimes she didn't volunteer that she *wasn't* white in order to provide us with what we needed.

It wasn't until we moved into the suburbs, where we were the only black folks, that it came into really sharp relief that we were hated. White folks tried to burn crosses, burn our house down, and there were death threats almost every day. We would go back to our old community on Sundays for church, where we were embraced, but the rest of the week we were hated.

I approached the research of my genealogy as a black woman—I *am* a black woman—so, yes, it was curious to me when I discovered how much white blood runs through my ancestry. It's interesting, too, because when I first started doing the genealogy work, I was met with incredible resistance by white folks in Louisiana, where I went to try to dig up various records. And now, it is a totally different reaction, in that everyone wants to help me find every branch, and when I give readings in Louisiana, people will stand in a very long line to tell me that we're part of the same family. Certainly the endorsement from Oprah Winfrey makes a difference, but also, I think, it demonstrates a willingness to see beyond what one might have first seen.

In *Cane River*, strength for these women—the women who bore me—began with one another. These women were not talking about whether to get a Lexus or a Mercedes. They were talking about prioritizing with respect to the real fundamentals of life, and I wanted to give them voice for that reason. Not only did they survive a time that I'm not sure I could have survived myself but they did it with different strategies, and they prioritized in terms of what was truly important. They didn't have twelve priorities, and the priorities they had were not frivolous. And all these priorities centered on the desire to make life better for their family. Today, when I think about where strength begins for me, I know that it began with these women. More specifically, it began with my mother. Her approach was always one of such survival, of making the best of what there was, of controlling the parts of the situation that she could.

When I thought about these women, I thought about myself, and how as a young girl I was walking to school and having people spit on me. To understand these women, I went back to that feeling of isolation and loneliness and tried to remember what it was that allowed me to get up and walk to school one more day. I learned to rely on myself, and I became very self-possessed, because outside the front door of my house was a consistently hostile place.

Chapter Two

MAGNIFICENT BARBARISM

> THEY USED TO HAVE A CERTAIN MAGNIFICENT BARBARISM
> ABOUT THEM THAT I LIKED. THEY WERE NEVER VULGAR,
> NEVER IMMORAL, BUT RATHER ROUGH AND PRIMITIVE,
> WITH AN UNCONVENTIONALITY THAT SPENT ITSELF IN
> LOUD GUFFAWS, SLAPS ON THE BACK, AND NAPS IN THE
> CORNER.
>
> —"Of the Meaning of Progress"

After our reunion in the summer of 1980, Tess and I made a trip to Boston, about an hour away from where she lived in Portsmouth, New Hampshire. She took me to the Boston Common, where, she told me, she'd met my birth father twelve years before, while he was playing guitar to anyone who would listen, but primarily to the pretty young white girls who would gather often and regularly to hear him play.

Later in the day, we walked a side street and passed three or four grown black men with broad shoulders and jet black skin. One or two wore sunglasses, one a leather jacket, while another's feet crushed down hard on the pavement with leaden brown boots. They struck me as viciously elegant, unsettlingly familiar, and outright dangerous. A couple of them directed overtures my way: "Hey, brown sugar"; "Hey there, little mama," they said, as if I were the girl cousin in their family that all the boy cousins wanted to kiss. I quickened my pace, bowed my head, and felt ashamed, embarrassed, and frightened.

"Oh, don't mind them," Tess said dispassionately. "They're just bored, jive black men."

As a girl who wanted desperately to please the mother who had given her away, and, almost as important, to appear sophisticated in her eyes, it struck me then that I should agree with her, whether I understood what she meant or not. Those men, I rationalized, were not actually trying to get a date with me, or to scare or hurt me; that they were simply acting out common, everyday black cultural behavior—common, everyday jive black cultural behavior? I didn't know for sure, but I certainly wasn't going to incriminate myself any further by asking Tess the difference. I knew that she already considered me terribly immature and vastly uninformed, particularly as a child who carried her DNA.

Still, I subsequently began to cultivate a belief that there might, in fact, be a difference between common black cultural behavior and common jive black cultural behavior. The point, though, then, as it is now perhaps, was not the difference in types of black cultural behavior, but the perception that a particular black cultural behavior existed at all. This perception was born, in part, out of general observation, such as that which Du Bois made of the Burkes, an uneducated Tennessee family that, as he described them, possessed "a certain magnificent barbarism." And, out of an observation, such as mine about the men in Boston, who, like the Burkes, evoked a kind of crude and unscathed sense of cultural purpose. To be black was to be nothing other than themselves and to be themselves was to be nothing other than black. The Burkes: "two brown and yellow lads, and a tiny haughty-eyed girl." The men in Boston: "bored, jive black men."

Stanley Crouch is widely known as an outspoken provocateur and a prolific writer of social commentary, as is evident in his articles, books, and essays. As a cultural figure, he both perpetuates and aggravates ideas about authentic blackness or any sort of assumed black behavior. He takes issue with the sort of thinking implied by Du Bois's "magnificent barbarism" remark—too loud, overly animated, decidedly raw, and unlearned—and, conversely, with that behavior introduced by the emergent Afrocentrist movement of the early 1990s, referring to said movement in a 1994 article for *City Journal* as another of the "clever but essentially simple-minded hustles that have come about over the last 25 years, promoted by what was once called 'the professional Negro'—a person whose identity' and 'struggle' constituted a commodity . . . [that] benefit[s] from the obsession with 'authenticity' of this mongrel nation of ours."

Crouch is nothing if not interesting, and he is someone who is able to look at race with an unflinching lack of sentimentality, which is elucidated in the following remark from his book *The All-American Skin Game*: ". . . ours is a time in which the conventions of 'blackness' encourage the simplifying of human experience in the interest of a half-baked 'unity.' "

Stanley Crouch

There's no question that Du Bois was a vastly talented and brave thinker. I just don't buy all of it. Du Bois was a summation of a very complex process that is usually not discussed and that I spend a good bit of space assessing in the book I did with Playthell Benjamin—*Reconsidering the Souls of Black Folk* [Running Press Book Publishers, 2003]—in which I chose to discuss the extraordinary moment and the process when black Americans and white abolitionists essentially purified the whole human concept of the enlightenment.

Initially, universal humanity meant only Europeans. There were no other terms. White Europeans and great thinkers like Hume and Voltaire, even though we cite them today as supreme intellectuals, had attitudes toward black people that were far from scientific, and actually pretty vile. And what is so fascinating to me is that black Americans had to reject some of the most advanced social ideas at that time, which included the idea of polygenesis, or multiple beginnings, and go back to the Bible, which taught one beginning—Eden—for all humankind. Black Americans had to reject those earlier ideas in order to go beyond the racially oriented stance that human beings began in different places and in different ways and that subsequently some were placed more highly than others in the social order. And that position, of course, could easily justify slavery. But to take on slavery with full thunder, black Americans had to propose a vision of universal humanism that had no boundaries.

Beyond that, as I make clear in *Reconsidering Souls*, I think white folks drove Du Bois crazy. I don't mean he needed to be in a mental institution, but I think he went off in the beginning of the 1930s. A lot of people disagree with me, but I think he reached a point where he essentially rejected his previous position and decided that since white America was not going to accept black people, then black people needed to resegregate. And that was the kind of thinking that led to his problems with the NAACP (the National Association for the Advancement of Colored

People). And, then, by the time he wrote that eulogy for Stalin ("On the Great Leader and Teacher," printed in *The National Guardian*, March 1953), you know he was gone. His defense of Stalin is indefensible and can easily be connected to how those on the Left have justified mass murder with the same verve that those on the Right have justified their heroes of mass slaughter.

I have thought about Du Bois in one way or another for many years. I'm fifty-seven now, but I read *The Souls of Black Folk* for the first time when I was in my teens, in an Afro-American history class that I took outside of high school. I was already involved in CORE (the Congress of Racial Equality) and picket lines and the civil rights movement in Los Angeles, protesting things like there not being any black supervisors in supermarkets. The only jobs that black people held at supermarkets were putting the groceries in bags. My parents weren't really involved, but they were supportive of my efforts.

The black teachers, and most of the white ones, too, who worked in the Los Angeles public schools I attended taught with missionary zeal, but they did not express the kind of intensity that Du Bois had. That sense was not there in any political sense—these teachers did not attempt to pass on any kind of rage; their focus was preparation for a world that might not treat you fairly because of your skin color. They wanted to supply you with the best tools necessary to create your own way, to handle your obstacles. They also wanted you to be so determined that you would not be spooked or broken if the white folks started dealing you your cards from the bottom of the deck. Somewhere inside themselves, the black teachers might have felt that red-hot part of Du Bois that comes out in the melodramatic piece of fiction in *The Souls of Black Folk*, "The Coming of John," but they didn't let their students know. I think they thought it might discourage us.

Du Bois was about something else—he was about pure expression of what was on his mind. In "The Coming of John," he's actually talking about something very specific, which is how a black person who had cultivated himself was still secondary to someone who was white:

> The great brown sea lay silent. The air scarce breathed. The dying day bathed the twisted oaks and mighty pines in black and gold. There came from the wind no warning, not a whisper from the cloudless sky. There was only a black man hurrying on with an ache in his heart, seeing neither sun nor sea, but starting as from a dream at the frightened cry that woke the pines, to see his dark sister struggling in the arms of a tall and fair-haired man.
>
> He said not a word, but, seizing a fallen limb, struck him with all the pent-up hatred of his great black arm; and the body lay white and still beneath pines, all bathed in sunshine and in blood. John looked at it dreamily, then walked back to the house briskly, and said in a soft voice, "Mammy, I'm going away,—I'm going to be free."

I know what was on Du Bois's mind all the time—that any redneck cracker thought he was superior merely because he was a cracker. Most people today, because of so much obvious black expertise, among other things, and because of contemporary television shows like *ER* and *The Wire*, to mention just two, can't even imagine that level of sustained stupidity and power based solely on color.

We do, however, have a strain of lunacy in mass media that is consistent with Du Bois's outrage in 1903, when *The Souls of Black Folk* was first published. And that strain is actually an extension of the minstrel shows. At a recent book party in New York, I met a young professional black woman who took the position that hip-hop performers like L'il Kim and other shameless black media sluts, thugs, and buffoons projected as supposedly being "authentic" black people are not, actually, the *real* black people. She meant that the L'il Kims of the world have nothing to do with a person such as herself, or the millions of other black women out there who are literate, sophisticated, responsible, and all of that—with plenty of soul in the mix.

In mass media, over and over, black people are defined in such a narrow way. One white guy, earnest as the day is long, once said to me that rap allows the modern-day white person to come into contact with the black person most removed from white society. Garbage. How is it that an ignorant, illiterate, crudely materialistic black person can be removed from the white world when that person comes straight out of the minstrel show? In other words, if you're looking at these Negroes with their "bling-bling," as they call it, their hideous jewelry—that's not new. That's what people were shown in the minstrel shows: the ignorant, tasteless, overdressed buffoon-level Negro forever impressed by glitter. If Du Bois were here right now, he and I would be on the same page when it comes to this garbage.

What we in America have to realize is that we have fallen into a decadent hole, all of us. When I was growing up in the fifties, the equivalent of hip-hop figures today, the so-called street brothers, they would get *no* conversation at all. An ignorant Negro like that—the "Hey, baby, you need to talk to me" Negro—zip. No play. But then during the sixties, this whole idea of black authenticity first began to emerge, and that's what really started to decimate people intellectually. Black authenticity has been narrowed in definition. All the teachers, doctors, lawyers, artists, engineers, politicians, college professors, career military types, and so on, have either been pushed out of the picture or dismissed, as "authenticity" has become more and more connected to suffering, which comes from the idea that the *real* people—black, white, and other— are down here in the mud; they're not up there, wherever up there is.

This is a purely American variation. A lot of movies in the thirties dealt with that—a wealthy man falls for a woman who's a commoner and his family can't deal with it, and so forth. Or some wonderful common guy from the bottom steals the heart of the girl from above. So, I feel like black folks are just playing that part out. It's a cultural paradigm. But the way that paradigm got twisted up in black America during the late sixties has had deadly consequences. In effect, the gangsta rapper—the so-called street brother—as sex symbol or as gritty *pure* male icon is actually just the black version of the white biker on a motorcycle with slicked-back hair who drove white girls crazy in the fifties after Marlon Brando dampened their panties in *The Wild One*.

By the late sixties and early seventies, certain things had come together. Naïve Black Nationalism and the Marxist sentimentality about "the proletariat" were unintentionally whipped together for the icing, and the cake got its recipe from Franz Fanon's celebration of "the fellah"—the Algerian "street brother" in *The Wretched of the Earth*. This led to middle-class black girls swooning over the Panthers, singing their own version of "I Want a Roughneck." Think about it. It's as clear as the summer sun.

But the question in all of this is: "Do I think there is such a thing as an authentic black person?" Yes, but I would imagine it would depend upon the context. If somebody is from Boston, his or her version of black authenticity is not the same as somebody's from Charleston, South Carolina. There are regional varieties of black Americans that no one ever acknowledges. Whenever people talk about black Americans, they always act as though there's this one factory, this one ethnic factory in Indiana or somewhere, that just churns us out.

I think of black folks collectively as being like a bicycle—it's one pedal up, one pedal down. That is to say, there is plenty to like and there's plenty that's extraordinary. There's also plenty that's not extraordinary, as with any group of people. These young black kids go around today using the word *nigga*, shouting it at the tops of their voices or blasting it out of their cars as they listen to rap—and that, bringing it back to Du Bois, is the barbarism without the magnificence. Seeking the magnificent should always be the point, whether it comes from above or from below.

Before this era of decadence, black people, from coast to coast, understood what Du Bois understood, which is that something could rise from this crude, illiterate group of people, and that that something, in every way possible, could gleam with eloquence, which is the highest form of human statement, regardless of style. No matter how badly things have gone or are going, don't count us out. We have come through even worse things and we will, I'm sure, come through this.

Chapter Three

A FUTURE WITH PROMISE

> HOW CURIOUS A LAND IS THIS—HOW FULL OF UNTOLD
> STORY, OF TRAGEDY AND LAUGHTER, AND THE RICH
> LEGACY OF HUMAN LIFE; SHADOWED WITH A TRAGIC
> PAST, AND BIG WITH FUTURE PROMISE!
>
> —"Of the Black Belt"

Up until the sixth grade, I wore and kept my hair as best I could—pulled back, braided, or under a scarf. My hair had never been properly cared for and was, consequently, at least in the back, a mess of snarls and mats. Tess, my birth mother, knew of a black hairdresser in Portsmouth, and less than a year after we had reunited, she wasted little time in scheduling an appointment.

Elease's salon smelled like hot metal, Vaseline, and hair spray. Small and lightless, it had a funky, colorless carpet, and plastic helmet-shaped hair dryers lined up on top of fake leather chairs along the walls and into the waiting area, where a squat brown Formica coffee table held outdated issues of *Ebony* and *Jet*. Tess and I waited as Elease went seriously about her business of jerry-curling and hot-combing, while a few suspicious glances spilled our way from the other women waiting or being serviced, particularly toward Tess, the only white woman there.

Elease gestured with a free hand, the other encased in a plastic glove smothered with straightening cream, for me to come over to her chair. I sat down reluctantly while she removed a glove, capped a jar, and rummaged around in a drawer for just the right tool. She dug her fingers into my thick, unkempt hair and summarily declared, "My goodness, girl, who on earth has been takin' care of this here hair?"

It marked the first time that my hair had been brushed out thoroughly and completely, and it was not a painless process. As a very young girl, long before I met Tess, when I still wore my hair in a simple untamed Afro, I had let only my father tend to it with a soft-bristled brush, which then, even I knew, had mainly just been a gesture. My kind of hair needed to be brushed with a hard-bristled brush and detangled thoroughly on a regular basis, then my scalp greased and my whole head wrapped at night, which I didn't know but which Elease sharply instructed. And, too, it had been a good thing that we'd come when we did, she declared on our way out the door, giving a reluctant and understated, yet entirely genuine, nod of credit aimed toward Tess.

I don't suppose Du Bois gave much thought to the treatment and grooming of black hair. Although it is clear from this chapter's epigraph—"How curious a land this is—how full of untold story, of tragedy and laughter, and the rich legacy of human life; shadowed with a tragic past, and big with future promise!"—that he did care about and respect those who rose up from adversity to succeed on their own terms. Whether or not these were terms that incorporated black hair care—and what is now, one hundred years later, one of the best-known, ritualistic, and often hotly debated legacies of black culture—may or may not matter.

Born to former slaves as Sarah Breedlove in 1867, Madam C J. Walker was orphaned, married, widowed, and a single mother by the age of twenty. Impoverished and with very little formal education, she supported herself and her daughter for eighteen years by working as a washerwoman in St. Louis, Missouri, before making a single and momentous observation that would lend value and credence to Du Bois's notion of "a tragic past . . . big with future promise!"

Through both her own experience and her attentiveness to that of others, Walker established that black hair, particularly black women's hair, required a different kind of product and maintenance from that of Caucasian hair.

In 1905, two years after the publication of *The Souls of Black Folk*, Walker's seemingly simple yet remarkably astute assessment resulted in the development of a hair product that would soon grow into a million-dollar business, bringing to light the concept of hair straighteners and hot combs, and transforming forever the modern aesthetic of black women in America.

Although there is so far no formal historical data that indicates how well Walker and Du Bois knew each other, there is evidence that, as contemporaries, the two corresponded briefly over issues of community activism and philanthropy. That evidence appears in the 1999 biography *On Her Own Ground: The Life and Times of Madam C. J. Walker,* written by Walker's great-great-granddaughter, A'Lelia P. Bundles.

Bundles, who for years resisted her connection to Walker because of the widely agreed-upon but wholly incorrect conjecture that Walker invented the hot comb, thereby promoting the straightening of black women's hair to effect a more white semblance, has said that her decision to write her great-great-grandmother's biography was due, in part, to the discovery that Walker was respected by the person who had been Bundles's cultural icon when she was growing up: W. E. B. Du Bois.

A'Lelia Bundles

When i was in college, at Harvard, I was in the stacks of Widener Library one day doing some research—I don't even remember what I was looking for, but somehow I ended up in the stacks—and discovered a shelf of books written by some of those European pseudo-scientists from the nineteenth century who believed that black people were inferior because our hair was like sheep's wool. In their twisted minds, that meant we were equivalent to animals. As it happened, somewhere near those books were bound issues of *The Crisis* (the magazine of the NAACP).

I flipped through a couple of volumes and came upon the August 1919 issue, which included an obituary of Madam C. J. Walker by W. E. B. Du Bois.

Now, at this point, I was somewhat ambivalent about being the great-great-granddaughter of Madam Walker. Having grown up in a family where my mother was vice president of the Walker Company and my father was president of another company that manufactured black hair care products, I knew the basic story, but I really didn't know the truth about Madam Walker. I was, in many ways, interpreting her through the lens of other people, and the lens that was the clearest, or so it seemed at that point, was the one that said Madam Walker had invented the straightening comb and wanted to make black people look white.

In high school during the late 1960s, when I wanted to express my blackness by having an Afro, my father and I had one of the most memorable standoffs of my teenage years. He said, "You know, boys are never going to look at you if you get an Afro, and how do you think we are going to pay for college if everyone wears an Afro?" and all that. When my father and I had this set-to about my hair, my mother, who was much wiser on this particular issue than my father, must have worked on him. Finally, he came around after I'd had a very vivid and violent nightmare about all this—about my struggle for personal expression. He had been traveling at the time, and when he learned of my nightmare, he called me from the road, and he said,

"Okay, you can have this Afro." I look back now and think, It's just hair, but at the time, it was so important to me.

A week or so later, my mother took me to the Walker Beauty School, and the students there rolled my hair up on permanent-wave rods and transformed my chemically straightened hair into this Angela Davis–size Afro. As a little girl, my hair was always long, and that made people tell me they thought I was cute, but when I got the Afro, that made me feel strong. And the truth is, I would take strong over cute any day, because strong is much more lasting.

At the time, I equated natural hair with strength, and from what others had said about Madam Walker, she was about straightening natural hair. So when I discovered Du Bois's obit in *The Crisis* that afternoon at Widener Library, it was a pivotal moment for me. You see, Du Bois had been my intellectual hero ever since I first read *The Souls of Black Folk* in high school. At the time, it was the most profound and nuanced treatment of race I had ever read. And, as an impressionable seventeen-year-old, it helped me to better understand the conundrum of race and identity. So, after reading the obit, I felt that if my intellectual hero thought there was some value in this woman, Madam Walker, and could see beyond what other people had said, then I needed to reexamine her. And that reexamination led to three decades of research about her, and a real admiration for what she accomplished.

One of my frustrations, though, especially as I was researching *On Her Own Ground,* is that I was never able to find any real body of correspondence between Madam Walker and Du Bois, so I still don't know the exact quality of their relationship. I do have a letter where he asks her to contribute to the Music School Settlement, and there are little signs here and there—including an invitation to his conference at Troutbeck—that indicate he respected her. Maybe it was her money and her ability to fund things that attracted him to her, but for someone who was as much of an elitist as Du Bois was, to recognize Madam Walker as a self-made woman who, as he said, helped "transform a race" is remarkable, and it made me see her in a different light.

Now, as we know, black people's hair has a history that can be both painful and humorous. Early in the twentieth century, hair became the tyranny of our existence: If your hair was not straight, if people saw the slightest evidence of your nappy hair, then they believed you wouldn't get a job, you wouldn't get married, and that you would be considered ugly. By the 1960s, the backlash, of course, was all about loving what had been so rejected and repressed. I think today we need to be more accepting of our style choices, and what we are born with, although I also understand the pain many people associate with childhood memories about hair. Many black women tell me horror stories about how their mothers were borderline abusive when they combed or pressed their hair. I know there is a lot of negative emotion associated with that, but I also think that sometimes we give hair more power than it deserves.

Madam Walker's initial goal was to help women heal scalp disease, which was very common at the time and was causing women to go bald. It's very hard for people to hear that, because what they think they know, as I thought I knew, is that Madam Walker invented the straightening comb. Over time, the myth about the hot comb took hold and was perpetuated by some Walker Company employees. But it's just not true.

What is important to me now is for people to understand that Madam Walker loved black people, and she used her wealth and influence to help her community as a philanthropist and political activist and as a supporter of Du Bois's antilynching movement. Her early life was difficult and tragic. She overcame obstacles and made a future for herself and others. She embodied the fact that as a people we played a key role in the making of America. We are more than slave history. She lived what Du Bois knew: that we must be taken seriously, that we deserve to be taken seriously, and that we are valuable . . . that we are a brilliant people.

Chapter Four

TO BE A PROBLEM

Between me and the other world there is ever an unasked question: unasked by some through feelings of delicacy; by others through the difficulty of rightly framing it. All, nevertheless, flutter round it. They approach me in a half-hesitant sort of way, eye me curiously or compassionately, and then, instead of saying directly, "How does it feel to be a problem?" They say, "I know an excellent colored man in my town . . ." To the real question, "How does it feel to be a problem?" I answer seldom a word.

—"Of Our Spiritual Strivings"

John was one of my best friends in high school. He was cute, athletic, book-smart, and popular. We'd been good friends since middle school, when I'd helped him through a rough breakup with Susie. At one point, shortly after the breakup, we made out at a school dance, but we were never boyfriend and girlfriend. We talked often on the phone and hung out together in between classes and at weekend parties. We were, though, very different people. He played soccer and skied; I did regional theater and wrote short stories. He wore sweaters from L. L. Bean, and, despite a valiant effort at conformity in middle school, in high school I dressed primarily in eclectic thrift shop garb. His father was a teacher and his mother was a stay-at-home mom, who may have dabbled in real estate—I don't remember; my parents were both artists. But, we were good friends, and we shared a solid mutual respect for each other.

When the sophomore prom came around, we were both unattached. Why not go together? we thought. No big deal. Everyone knew we were just friends.

I don't know how word got around so fast, but the next morning when I got to school, halfway down the main hall a friend stopped me, wearing a grieved expression.

"What?" I asked.

"Have you heard?"

"Heard what?"

Apparently, John's parents were not thrilled about the idea of their son taking a black girl to the prom, and rumor had it they'd issued a firm warning that if he did go with me, no pictures would be taken. This was odd, because my friends often and regularly told me that they didn't even think of me as black.

John and I went to the prom. No pictures were taken. And although John did later concede that his parents were uncomfortable with him taking a black girl to the prom, we did not discuss the issue further or bring it up again.

This memory and experience is marked for me in the opening words of the first essay in *Souls*, "Of Our Spiritual Striving": "Between me and the other world there is ever an unasked question: unasked by some through feelings of delicacy; by others through the difficulty of rightly framing it. All, nevertheless, flutter round it. . . . To the real question, 'How does it feel to be a problem?' I answer seldom a word." I have wondered throughout my life how many times my friends have wanted to ask me how it felt to be a problem—or would they or I even have known to recognize my condition, my general presence, as such?

Du Bois's reflection comes from witnessing the silent disbelief of his white friends and colleagues, who recognized his intelligence and the behavior that mirrored their own but who were unable to reconcile the color of his skin, given what they thought they knew about black people. It is an insight that led to an affecting discovery for the scholar and activist David Graham Du Bois, whose mother, Shirley Graham, married W. E. B. Du Bois when David Graham was in his late teens. David Graham admired his stepfather deeply and aspired to emulate Du Bois, only to realize that a likeness to his role model meant the reality of "being a problem."

David G. Du Bois

Growing up, I was conscious in my associations with white people that for some reason I was identified as different. "You're different," white people would say. The implication, of course, was that they could be my friend and I could be their friend because I wasn't like other black people. There's no way to know what the qualifying factor was, although my assumption is that my behavior, whatever it may have been, was not "normal" for black people. And, yet, how would they know? That is what is at the heart of the intense separation between blacks and whites that has characterized American society from its very beginning.

I was raised by my grandparents—a Methodist minister and his wife—and *The Crisis* was a staple in our home. Du Bois had, in fact, visited our home before I was born, when my mother was still a young girl. He had come to Portland, Oregon, for a lecture engagement, and, of course, hotels weren't taking black folks back then, so he stayed with the minister and his wife, my grandparents, at the parsonage. That's when my mother and Du Bois first met.

I did not meet him personally until many years later, when I got out of the army and moved to New York City, where I enrolled at Hunter College. My mother and Du Bois were regular companions by this point. He had recently returned to New York from Atlanta because of troubles he was having with the Atlanta University trustees. He returned to New York as research director of the NAACP. I don't recall the exact occasion when we met, but I do remember having revered him so much that meeting him was one of those sorts of things you don't believe is happening to you.

There were so many people who greatly admired Du Bois, and who demonstrated this admiration all the time, that, of course, I felt tremendously honored to be in such close proximity to him. I observed his manner, his way, everything about him. I didn't particularly try to emulate him, although I did want to emulate his conviction and commitment. He was not always serious, as some might think. He had a very present, very cutting sense of humor, and he used it, especially when he was dealing with my mother. My mother was a very passionate, intense person. She could also be a very impatient, uptight person, and Du Bois constantly used humor as a way to calm her down. He made jokes out of things that she could get furious about. Du Bois was, though, basically a shy person, and so in his general interactions, his humorous side was not often revealed.

I lived with them, my mother and Dr. Du Bois, in their Brooklyn Heights home for about a year when I was in graduate school at New York University, although much of that time they were traveling abroad. When they were home, though, they would have guests in for dinner. They entertained regularly, and it was during intimate circumstances like this—because my mother did not invite people over with whom Du Bois did not feel relaxed and comfortable—that his humor would come out. And, too, the conversations were not always about race and politics.

Now, my mother, she was always thinking about politics. Whereas, Du Bois, because he was a highly disciplined person, wanted to relax at the end of his workday. At this time, his office was in their home, and we would all eat breakfast together in the morning, sometimes outside on the patio. Then he would go to his office and be gone all day. He might come out for a light lunch, or sometimes not, but either way, at the end of the day, when he was finished with his work, he was finished with his work.

My mother, having been denied his company all day

while he was in his office, was ready to come to him with all kinds of things to discuss, and that would sometimes produce friction. When he was working, his level of commitment and dedication was exhausting. My mother did have her own friends and colleagues, but to a large extent, their circle of friends centered on Du Bois.

My relationship with Du Bois was not very close. Apart from that year I lived with them, our paths did not cross much. Later, after I got married and moved to Harlem, we would sometimes see each other at meetings or functions, but I did not have the kind of relationship with him that I think people assume I had, or that even I wish I'd had. I don't know that I wished it so much, actually, because I was very concerned about not creating a problem for him. I didn't want to get in the way, so to speak. A couple of times, I did approach him with regard to my graduate work, which was in western hemisphere history, the closest I could get, at that time, 1950, to studying black history.

I was thinking about researching the reactions of black newspapers to the Populist movement of the 1890s for my thesis, and during my discussion with Du Bois about this idea, he pointed out that there was a black farmers' alliance that existed at that time, with over a million members. And, he said, it was an area of research and scholarship that should be looked at, because very little had so far been written about it. Du Bois felt this would be an area in which I could make a major contribution. I agreed, but I decided to wait and pursue it later as a subject for my doctorate instead. That was the only time, really, when I had that kind of interaction with Dr. Du Bois. When I went to him for advice, which I very seldom did, his approach was to ask questions that would help me to determine what I thought, so that I could make the decision on my own.

Du Bois never adopted me legally. I told him that I would like to have his name, and that I would like to consider him my father, and he was very welcoming and pleased about that. In lectures that I deliver now, I make the distinction that in the West African tradition, there is no such thing as a stepchild or a stepfather, and so, in that context, I consider myself the son of W. E. B. Du Bois, because he considered me his son. And that's it.

I was not particularly close with my mother, either. As I said, my grandparents raised me. And later on, when my mother and I began to develop a relationship as adults, it was fraught with difficulties. We became closest after Dr. Du Bois's death, and she was forced to leave Accra because of the coup against Nkrumah. She moved to Cairo, where I was living at the time, and I found her a home there. For a few years, we were constantly together, and were able to interact like mother and son. I didn't resent the fact that she left me to be raised by my grandparents, but I did have to come to terms with it over time.

One of the last conversations I had with my mother before she died had to do with my birth father. I had been told that my brother and I were taken away from him because he endangered our lives, but the truth of his existence and who he was as a person was something of a mystery, and it did come between my mother and me. In Cairo, finally, when we knew she was dying, I decided to raise the issue with her: "Tell me about my father." It was a very quiet, moving, very significant moment. My mother hesitated for a very long while, and then all she said was, "McCants"—that was his name, McCants—"was more sinned against than sinner." She didn't say another word. She didn't need to say another word.

When Du Bois died, he left everything to my mother, and when my mother died, she left everything to me. And so here I am, grateful to be carrying the legacy, a large part of which entails continuously reminding people of how much we can learn from reading *The Souls of Black Folk* today, because it tells us so much about race, and the idea of color as a determinant. Each of us lives in a limited time period of human existence, and although black Americans learned a great deal from the civil rights movement— things to do and things not to do—we're still coming out of the backlash that that movement precipitated. What we're going through right now, especially in entertainment and sports—the two areas in which we are permitted to be recognized—in terms of excessive promotion and so forth, is all part and parcel of the backlash. It is hard to find a positive black reaction to what is going on for us right now, but I know that it is there. It's beginning to emerge.

People of color make up some 75 percent of the world's population, and those are the same people who for the past four centuries have been the victims of European colonialism, imperialism, and exploitation—Africans and African Americans more than others, but all people of color from Asia, South America, Central America, the islands. It is inevitable that this situation will be reversed. It is happening as we speak. In 1915, Du Bois declared, "Most men in this world are colored. A belief in humanity means a belief in colored men. The future world will in all reasonable probability be what colored men [and women] make it." This is what Du Bois saw. This is where he got his strength.

Chapter Five

SIMPLE BEAUTY

> . . . THE VAGUE DREAM OF RIGHTEOUSNESS, THE MYSTERY
> OF KNOWING; BUT TO-DAY THE DANGER IS THAT THESE
> IDEALS, WITH THEIR SIMPLE BEAUTY AND WEIRD INSPIRA-
> TION, WILL SUDDENLY SINK TO A QUESTION OF CASH
> AND A LUST FOR GOLD.
>
> —"Of the Wings of Atalanta"

Like most normal teenage girls, I was pretty obsessed with boys during high school and the early years of college. Because those years also coincided with the onset of my racial consciousness, and because the only black relation I've ever known to be authentic is a black man, my birth father, I have subsequently made heavy association between blackness and men.

My black birth father existed in a world frozen in time, 1960s America, when he was identified and stereotyped by popular culture and the media for both the danger and allure of his alleged sexual prurience. All I ever heard about him from Tess was that he was a player, a womanizer, aiming to cross over and sell out, using every bit of what labeled him in the first place—that he seduced white women with his suave looks and muscular build, passing smoothly through and among them as some sort of trophy buck. My birth mother also told me that all my birth father ever really wanted was fame and wealth. Neither of which, sadly, did he ever achieve.

In the essay "Of the Wings of Atalanta," Du Bois considers variants of the "vague dream of righteousness" and the "simple beauty and weird inspiration" within the black world, and the chillingly predictive risk of downfall at the hands of lust and greed. As if to say: A genuine flicker of righteousness, a spell of indescribable splendor, and a jolt of the innately provocative existence of black people could and would disappear in seconds if those within the culture did not fast and accurately add these factors up to create a foundation—a foundation that would not yield to temptation.

Using the genre of magical realism—a genre that weaves realism and surrealism through narrative prose—writer Touré creates rich and powerful stories about black life that recognize and celebrate the factors Du Bois encouraged us to build upon a hundred years ago. Touré, who has said that he has been more so influenced by fiction than historical nonfiction, is an apostle of Du Bois not merely because he is a storyteller of tales righteous, beautiful, and weird but also because he, as Du Bois would have asked of any black man of his time, is a man who lives in the world he has created.

Touré

i'm more about fiction than sociology. *The Souls of Black Folk* has never spoken to me in the same way that great works of fiction have. Books like *Invisible Man*, *Their Eyes Were Watching God*, and *Song of Solomon* are books I have fallen really hard for, like a lover. While I'm reading the book, I'm having the relationship, and it can feel like romantic love. But I think everybody gets a sense of what's inside of *Souls*, because there've been so many books inspired by it and so many people moved by it. The book has been discussed and quoted so much, it's something that's in the air.

The magic realism that I use in *The Portable Promised Land* and my novel, *Soul City*, is a way of expressing blackness through my eyes. I see black people as so fresh and beautiful without even trying to be that I need a magic-tinged reality in my fiction to get all the beauty I see onto the page. When I walk around Fort Greene, Brooklyn, where I live, there's a large group of us—a lot of black artists and black artistic people, people with style and self-confidence. People walking down the street with some amazing strut, or some amazing outfit, not reacting to the white gaze at all. That's our creativity, thought, money, time, and ingenuity all coming together to make this beautiful presentation of blackness. The way for me to explain that on the page is through magic—to exaggerate so that you can see all the beauty I see. My writing is certainly a reaction to black culture throughout its history, and throughout the country, but it's also the specific, textural, and tangible relationship I have with the blackness I see in Fort Greene.

The way I first learned to write and interpret the world was through writing record reviews and then features, primarily for *Rolling Stone*, but also in other places. I always saw my job as expanding the complexity of the discussion of black hip-hop heroes. I knew they were deeper, more intelligent, more important, and more meaningful than they were being portrayed as in much of the media. Because I've been writing for *Rolling Stone*, I've been able to write about the kings of the industry—Tupac, Biggie, Snoop,

D'Angelo, DMX, Jay-Z, 50 Cent. I've been fortunate to have this vantage on the industry for a few years.

When I'm interviewing these people, I am always wanting them to go deeper on what made them become who've they've become. You can't just tell me, "Yeah, I'm the greatest." I try to get them to analyze themselves, and to talk about the influences that made them who they are. That's sometimes difficult in hip-hop, because nobody ever recognizes the influences. It's always "It's just me. I'm this good on my own." I don't know why that is.

The biggest problem I ever had was with Mary J. Blige—back during her *My Life* album. She was angry at everyone back then. But I also think she saw me as just this middle-class black kid from the *New York Times*, which I was then writing for, asking her questions that were just a little deeper than she wanted to go. Plus, we were in a limo going to the projects where she came from, which I think probably heightened the situation. But generally, there are never any problems. Part of the job of a journalist is to insinuate yourself into their world, to become one of the guys really quickly.

In my fiction, I want to entertain in the most vaunted sense of the word. I want to tell the most interesting stories possible. It's a performance to me. In *Soul City*, I created a dominantly black city somewhere in America, a place where people are filled with magic, because I wanted to create a world in which white people are on the outside. They are central to so many of us so much of the time. But if you can throw off the white gaze, it's an amazing experience. I mean, you need to get to a place where, if you feel like you want to have watermelon, just really feel like having that particular fruit, then you can walk into the middle of the Ritz and say, "Hey, man, I really just feel a need for watermelon deep in my soul." And you know the white people at the next table are thinking, There go those Negroes with their watermelon again, but you don't care. You can eat that watermelon at the Ritz without caring one bit. That's fun. I don't personally like watermelon, but that's not the point. You have to rid yourself of the notion that what white people think or do is going to inform who you are or the way you act or dress. I don't think that's delusional; I think it's delusional to go the other way. You'd go insane. Although I suppose many already have. I'm offering a panacea to that insanity.

I'm offering a world in my fiction that is primarily run and controlled by black people, where black people are central. They have problems, but their world does not fall apart in the end. This is not a political suggestion, or a prescription for modern America; it is a trip to a place that I have painted—a trip to Soul City. What I'm really trying to do, both in my work and in my life, with the subject of race is not to address it as a struggle, or a sociological issue, but, rather, as something cultural, something beautiful, something spiritual. It goes without saying that many black characters that appear in literature are not portrayed in a positive light. The characters in my work are happy and proud. They wear their blackness like a gold star.

It will be interesting to see what place race will have in our country as we move forward. Of course, it's still a huge issue, and still divides us in so many ways, but now, in this decade, there are tremendous national issues that didn't exist in the last decade. I think the issues of biracial Americans will become louder as time goes on, as that group grows larger and speaks about the complexity of race from their dual or multiple perspectives. I also see the issues of Arab Americans coming to the fore in a new way. Right now, they are the number-one niggers in America. I know a lot of black people who feel very literally like the noose has been loosened a little, as in: It's a little less likely for me to get stopped while I'm driving my car, because I'm not Arab.

Don't worry, black folks will go back to being the number-one niggers in America in due time. I have no doubt that the title will be retained. But, you know, for now, it's like the heavyweight champion was knocked out by an upstart. Who would have thought it possible? For once, niggas ain't the niggers of America. After four hundred consecutive years at number one, black folks are suddenly number two.

Chapter Six

PLAYING WITH MIGHTY FIRES

> To stimulate wildly weak and untrained minds is to play with mighty fires; to flout their striving idly is to welcome a harvest of brutish crime and shameless lethargy in our very laps. The guiding of thought and the deft coordination of deed is at once the path of honor and humanity.
>
> —"Of the Training of Black Men"

The University of New Hampshire had not been my first choice, but it was the only school that had provided me with enough financial aid so that I could afford to attend college at all. There were approximately ten thousand students at UNH at the time, about thirty-three of whom were black. It was a confusing time for me, because while I felt mostly uninspired by the university and its surroundings, I had also begun for the first time to struggle openly with my racial identity.

Up until then, there had been experiences, issues, run-ins, and incidents that made it quite clear how other people perceived my racial identity, but I had never taken it on myself, or decided what it meant to me. My first year of college seemed a good time to do that, and while I had dated a few black boys during summers with my birth mother throughout high school, I had taken a lot of heat from those boys about the authenticity of my blackness.

From stories my birth mother told me about the 1960s, I formed a vague notion that being black might entail being politically active somehow, thereby prompting my decision to resurrect the university's black student union. The organization was in its twentieth year of a self-imposed hiatus—which began in 1969—when I began canvassing the basketball team, which shamelessly comprised more than half the thirty-three black students who attended UNH. It didn't occur to me that most, if not all, of the guys on the basketball team were at the university in the first place because they could play ball, not because they were political activists, or that they might not have the slightest interest in issues surrounding race on any kind of intellectual level. I decided I was going to make a new kind of political organization, one that didn't necessarily demand that we fight battles or anything quite that serious, but, rather, one that allowed black students just to hang out and be black. All a black student union requires is black students, right?

As it turned out, the guys on the basketball team were not having it. Mainly, they didn't want to take the inherent risk of getting into trouble by being involved with an ostensibly activist organization and then losing their scholarships. I did manage, though, to get several of them to participate, and by midyear we had our first meeting, which was almost pitifully bad and unorganized. I had no idea what I was talking about. But I pressed on, and for the second meeting I invited the man I remember as the university's only black professor, Troy Davis, my adviser and mentor, to speak to us and help give us some direction.

Professor Davis, a strong, sane pillar of a man, told us that there wasn't just one way to be black, and that there had been a powerful lot of pain and suffering and action before we came along that allowed for this as a possibility. He said that we could decide how we wanted to fight from here on out, but that there would be fighting ahead—that, we could be sure of. He told us that being black didn't mean playing basketball, or being militant, or treating women badly, or skipping classes, or placing excessive value on material things, or even being a member of a black student union. He told us to learn about ourselves, to get an education, and to resist apathy. If we were able to do all that, he said, and could then translate that into the mission of a black student collective, it would be a good day.

Later that year, I spoke on behalf of the black student union at a diversity conference hosted by the university; NAACP chairman Julian Bond was the keynote speaker. His elegance was astounding, and a small hustle of hope danced around him with effortless charisma. He spoke so plainly and so clearly about the struggle for equality and how to remain engaged. But he was cautionary as well, in a way that reminded me of Du Bois's suggestion from "Of the Training of Black Men"—that to "stimulate wildly weak and untrained minds is to play with mighty fires; to flout their striving idly is to welcome a harvest of brutish crime and shameless lethargy in our very laps." It also reminded me of my efforts with the boys on the basketball team. While my intention may have been pure, my approach was naïve and artless.

The central theme in what was being said by Professor Davis, Julian Bond, and Du Bois in terms of generating a sustained force to be reckoned with is about knowing yourself and understanding how you are connected to the greater, more universal war to be waged, because, as Du Bois portended, "The guiding of thought and the deft coordination of deed is at once the path of honor and humanity."

Julian Bond

All throughout *The Souls of Black Folk*, Du Bois places an emphasis on the kind of classical, exalted education that he received—a kind of rigid education, from his childhood classrooms in New England to his time at Harvard and in Berlin. I think he believed that untrained, uneducated black people were weak. Not weak in the sense that early eugenics promoted—that black people were inherently less than human—but weak in the sense that they were less than well prepared for the modern day of his time. Although it is clear that Du Bois felt blacks should be given the same kind of education he had received, based on his own high opinion of himself, I think he also knew that wasn't going to happen. He encouraged, then, a sort of decent median education, one that he felt would allow black people to come to an understanding about the world in which they lived and a way to contend with it.

What struck me the most about *The Souls of Black Folk* when I first read it in college was Du Bois's command of the language, and his ability to put one word after another and have the end result be so magnificent. I remember feeling a kind of envy almost, and hope, too, that if I extended myself far enough, I could maybe come close to that, because I was interested in being a writer and I admired felicitous writing. So when I read *Souls* for the first time, it was less about the thoughts and more about the language. I did find the writing a little flowery in places, but I also associated it with an earlier time and an earlier style. It wasn't something I wanted to copy, but it was something I wanted to emulate.

When I began to consider the thoughts as opposed to the writing in *Souls*, or maybe the thoughts and the writing together, it was a confirmation of the ideas I had thought about and believed in but which I had not been able to articulate, or at least not in such a commanding fashion. I've always been interested in words and the way they can sway people, change their minds, and *Souls* was the perfect example of how that's done—this combination of tale and truth, story and fact. It wasn't something I sat around and talked about with my friends, although it was a book that people were reading at the time, not, perhaps, as an assignment, but out of general interest. I was never in a setting where I could say, "What did you think about what Du Bois said on page twenty-six of *The Souls of Black Folk?*"

My father knew Du Bois, and I have a photograph of him with Du Bois and E. Franklin Frazier, commissioning my sister and me to a life of scholarship. So when I read the book, I knew that this great man had been in my presence, but I was three years old at the time and have no memory of this, just the photograph to remind me. I did know he had been around me, around my life, and that the effect of the things he did were also all around me. I lived on black college campuses all of my life, and he was a part of that world. I felt not a kinshp, but certainly a kind of relationship with him.

His prophesy about the color line resonated for me then as it does now, and the only difference between my reaction then and now is that now the color line is the problem not of the twentieth century but of the twenty-first century. I became active in the civil rights movement when I was twenty years old, right around the same time I read *Souls*. Although I can't say the book is what *propelled* me into the movement, it did coincide and remain as a reference for me. Not that it was something I thought about every day—Well, Du Bois said something about this—but just as a kind of distant reference. I didn't read anything else of his until much later on, and so *The Souls of Black Folk* was him for me. The book, vis-à-vis Du Bois, existed in my life in a sort of guardianship capacity.

At twenty years old, I wasn't thinking, I'm going to tackle the problem of the color line, but as the movement was bursting out around me, I was thinking that I was going to take the problem on in some way. I was going to take it on, other people around me were going to take it on, people before me had taken it on, and people after me would take it on—each and all, with no end in sight. It's an ongoing struggle. Even if racial discrimination disappeared tomorrow morning, there would still be work to be done, because you would then see as clearly as ever the divisions—economic, political, and otherwise—that race prejudice has caused. If racism were to end, society would still be maladjusted. As it does not appear that racism will end, however, you have to look at things over the long term and consider the progress on a continuum.

Every time you say, "Progress has been made," you recognize that in some ways the current expression of the problem makes it more difficult to surmount than did the old expression of the problem. Nonetheless, change has occurred, laws have been passed, advances have been noted and registered, things are not now as they were forty years ago, and in many respects, they're better as a general proposition than they were, which lends encouragement that forty years hence, they can be even better. Having seen the past change, you can foresee the future change. And that's what the NAACP is about. It's sort of self-reinforcing as an organization—we conduct a battle, we win that battle, we acknowledge that we accomplished something, and then we move on to something else. Or we think, Here's an old battle we haven't won yet, and we could still win. There are enough victories to keep hope alive, and that's what activism is.

In the broad sense, Du Bois was an activist—he helped direct the NAACP in its early organizational stages; he believed by calling together and participating in the Pan-African Congress that African liberation would result. What could be more difficult to have imagined at that time than African liberation? He not only imagined it; he believed it. I think activists range from the person who goes around his neighborhood organizing a protest against the city's failure to put up a stop sign at a danger-ous intersection, to someone who writes a polemic that others read and which then encourages them to take ac-tion, and Du Bois certainly fits into the latter category.

If Du Bois were here today, he would be critical of the NAACP, because Du Bois was a critic. I think he would say that *The Crisis* is not what it was when he was the ed-itor, and that the literary level is not as high. And it isn't. And it isn't going to be, but he'd say it anyway. If he were to look at the larger NAACP, all twenty-two branches, he'd probably say, "You know, a great number of these branches aren't doing anything; they're just having banquets." And he'd be absolutely right. Each branch of the NAACP is supposed to be the frontline troops for the civil rights movement in its respective community, and some branches just are not. But, of course, the NAACP is a volunteer-based organization, and working with volunteers is like herding cats. You can't *make* them do anything.

Du Bois set a very high standard for himself and for those around him. My parents told me as an adult that when Du Bois came to visit us when I was three years old and that picture was taken, he carried a pillow with him, which I thought odd. When I think of someone carrying his own pillow, I think of schoolgirls on airplanes. It's a little girlie. Nonetheless, he remains an endlessly compelling figure to me.

Chapter Seven

A PLACE IN THE WORLD

> HE BEGAN TO HAVE A DIM FEELING THAT, TO ATTAIN HIS
> PLACE IN THE WORLD, HE MUST BE HIMSELF, AND NOT
> ANOTHER. FOR THE FIRST TIME HE SOUGHT TO ANALYZE
> THE BURDEN HE BORE UPON HIS BACK, THAT DEAD-
> WEIGHT OF SOCIAL DEGRADATION PARTIALLY MASKED BE-
> HIND A HALF-NAMED NEGRO PROBLEM.
>
> —"Of Our Spiritual Strivings"

Michael is nearly the same color as I am. We could easily
have been siblings, based on the uncanny sameness of our
skin color alone, except that he has wildly sweet green eyes,
while mine are just a simple brown. A few months into our relationship, there was an important event. It was the opening
night of a play written by a woman from our small group of

black friends at Hampshire College, where I had recently trans-ferred from the University of New Hampshire. I had known about the event for a while. We had all known about it, and everyone had planned to go. When the evening came around, though, I suddenly had a million reasons for not going, which was odd, because I really had been looking forward to it. We had all been looking forward to this in particular.

Michael was supportive over the phone when I told him I couldn't go after all—too much homework—but as soon as I hung up the phone in the hallway of my dorm, I didn't feel quite right—like when you know the flu is coming on and your skin starts to ache and pull, your eyes feel scratchy and unfo-cused, and your blood rushes to small places of undiagnosed pain as your whole body fights against it instinctively.

Back in my room, I realized in an awkward, almost dis-turbing moment of clarity that for the past fifteen minutes I had been searching for images of black people in the pages of a magazine I was flipping through and that when I found one, I paused momentarily, feeling anxious and abandoned. I went out into the hall to call Michael. I knew he wouldn't be there. I knew he was at the play, and that made me panic. I left a message for him, hung up the phone, and then called again and left another message.

I went back to my room and tried to relax, but I couldn't. I wondered if I could still make it to the play, but my car had broken down the week before, the buses ran irregularly, and I wasn't even altogether certain where the play was being staged. I called Michael again and left another message, this message more frantic than the last, asking him to call me back as soon as he got home. I cried, wrote in my journal, changed my clothes twice, and listened to Roberta Flack over and over and over again until the hall phone rang and I raced out to get it.

Michael was there in minutes and listened attentively as I told him with wet eyes and a choked voice that I knew I had made a grave mistake in judgment, that I never should have missed Cara's play. I didn't know why I had decided not to go, but I would never forgive myself for missing it, because I knew, I just knew in my gut, that I should have been there, and that what that night had represented was a roomful of familiar, warm brown and black people appreciating and supporting one another by supporting one of our own. It felt like the last opportunity on the planet for me to sign up for that club—the black club. And, in a way, it was.

By not going, I was staking the claim, however subconsciously, of not being a member of any club, and I began, in words that were Du Bois's but that I could not have articulated better, "to have a dim feeling that, to attain [my] place in the world, [I] must be [my]self, and not another." It was the first time I understood not only how alone we all are in the world but also how alone I was on the subject of defining my blackness. It was both freeing and terrifying.

In the context of *Souls*, Du Bois is referring to the newly freed slave, who "for the first time . . . sought to analyze the burden he bore upon his back, that dead-weight of social degradation partially masked behind a half-named Negro problem." The paradox of being free and yet still weighed down by governing social forces is exactly how I felt that night in my dorm room.

In her work as a curator for the Whitney Museum and the Studio Museum of Harlem, Thelma Golden has actualized this very sense of irony through exhibitions, including "The Black Male," "Freestyle," and "Black Romantic." Each show offered piercingly poignant images of an apparently uniform black-ness, while Golden's own unique style allowed one to see a rich self-determination and a daringly original autonomy in these images.

Thelma Golden

W. E. B. Du Bois's idea of double consciousness ruled my college life. I went to Smith College in the 1980s, when the Art History Department did not teach black artists, and the African American Studies Department did not teach art. So I was constantly moving between the two departments, because I had this vision, so amorphous at the time, that I wanted to devote my life to black artists, and I didn't quite know how to make that happen. But the idea to make it happen came together when I read *The Souls of Black Folks*.

Du Bois allowed for this idea that artists, or artisans, can answer for themselves, and position their work as something that not only tells their story but reveals the conflict inherent in telling one's story. In the time since *Souls* was first published, we have seen that happen with African American artists: from where Du Bois began with the idea that all black people can speak for themselves, to a place where black artists embraced the notion that they could make work about anything, to the kind of moment we're in now—a more conceptual approach, one that digs even deeper into the understanding of what it is to be black.

You look at the artist Edward Bannister from the late 1800s, and these beautiful Hudson River landscapes that he painted—and again, this goes back to the idea of double consciousness—and you can see that at a certain level he was trying to prove legitimacy in the accepted art form, but at the same time, he was denying his other story as a black man making paintings in the late 1800s. In retrospect, though, there's also a freedom that is so intrinsic to a kind of black cultural thinking. "Black Romantic," the exhibition I mounted in 2002, was all about that, but it was about that in the extreme. The reason I did that exhibition was because of this question of not just what do black artists do but what they *should* do.

The artists I am most closely associated with, whose work interests me the most, are those artists who have taken a very personal approach to deciding how they will speak, and that individual voice is often controversial because of where it comes from. "Black Romantic" was about something else. It was about the "should" aspect. I've long been in the midst of these big debates about what the roles of black artists should be, and I've always been on the side where artists are saying, "Our role is to make the art that we're called to make. It is not to educate, to teach, or to uplift." But, out there in the world, there's a whole group of black artists who believe artwork should play a role in uplifting the race, and that it should do that by presenting images that are positive, images that display black culture in a way that it would like to be understood and that exhibits control over image making. Such work is incredibly sentimental, for it presents some ideal of a shared black past that doesn't really exist for anyone.

The work in "Black Romantic" was not kitsch, which was hard, too, in putting together this exhibition, because in the art world there's always this kind of high-low dichotomy that's being played out. But that wasn't the case here. This was serious artwork that had been seriously conceived. In terms of its point of view, however, it came from a place that was not conceptual. In some cases, it was political, but political, again, in terms of this idea of what a black artist is supposed to be. I did the exhibition because I felt that these two kinds of work—sentimental and conceptual—need to meet in the minds of the people who are looking at it.

I don't know if I could make the kind of exhibition

that would, say, reflect the souls of black folk in America, because I think that kind of show would require a sweeping view of black America, which I don't have. And, too, I'm not able to look at art that way. I know that there are these crass project exhibitions, like "Songs of My People," that purport to reflect the souls of black folk. But it's precisely that kind sweeping gesture that attempts to encapsulate the culture that I don't think is possible. During Black History Month, a lot of museums bring out their paintings by black artists and title the shows vaguely from the chapters of *The Souls of Black Folk*. The impetus for such shows really does speak to this idea of just how iconic the book is, but despite its iconic status, there is still a lack of understanding of the subtlety of Du Bois's argument.

I do think, though, that many of the questions Du Bois presented in *The Souls of Black Folk* have been answered in the work of black artists. When I think of his question, "How does it feel to be a problem?" I think of Adrian Piper's work from the eighties. The question of double consciousness plays out in the abstract work of any number of black artists—the way in which they have melded a European sensibility with black improvisational form. There is something in Du Bois's Pan-Africanism that speaks to the way in which various art movements have become globally connected. The Studio Museum in Harlem was founded with the idea of presenting African American art, but we are now interested in black art from all around the world. So that as much as Kara Walker sits in my brain every day, so does Chris Ofili. There's as much of Du Bois in Chris Ofili's sensibility as there is in Kara's.

For a long time, people felt a desire to write the story of black art, and that story was a chronological one—this begot this; this begets that—creating a lineage that would allow people to understand. I think that story is done being written. The major signposts are out there, and so in many ways I've tried to work around preconceived ideas by putting together work that spans continents, various media, and diverse ideas, because that's when art speaks fully to the complexity of black culture.

Chapter Eight

SELF-REALIZATION

> . . . WHEN TO EARTH AND BRUTE IS ADDED AN ENVIRON-
> MENT OF MEN AND IDEAS, THEN THE ATTITUDE OF THE
> IMPRISONED GROUP MAY TAKE THREE FORMS—A FEELING
> OF REVOLT AND REVENGE; AN ATTEMPT TO ADJUST ALL
> THOUGHT AND ACTION TO THE WILL OF THE GREATER
> GROUP; OR, FINALLY, A DETERMINED EFFORT AT SELF-
> REALIZATION AND SELF-DEVELOPMENT DESPITE ENVIRON-
> ING OPINION.
>
> —"Of Booker T. Washington and Others".

"Well then," she said, hands on hips, "you need to choose."
Katherine could be fierce when she wanted to be, and she
could make you feel about two feet tall in less than five seconds. She was beautiful, manipulative, brown-skinned, and an-

gry. Biracial, like me, she had also grappled with her identity, and with a way in which to present herself to the world that was both slightly intimidating but essentially unthreatening. We found each other at a time and in a place where we both felt deeply compromised, lonely, arrogant, and very much as though we had nothing to lose.

In my three years at Hampshire College, I had cultivated friendships with both white students and black students. The friendships were separate. The social scenes were separate. The expectations were separate. This posed small problems here and there, but for the most part, I'd been able to make it work, until my last year, when there was a sit-in by the black students and students of color, complete with a list of demands for the administration regarding diversity in the student body and faculty.

My boyfriend at the time, Michael, was a leader in the sit-in. All the black students loved him for many reasons, but mostly because he could negotiate with white folks so well. He was eloquent, elegant, a poet, a writer, a man without a father, who loved his mother fiercely. He made every minute count, every conversation intelligent, and every argument fair. His anger, though, was palpable. I had not seen him in the capacity of activist during the year we had been together, and his behavior at the sit-in scared me a little.

I didn't participate in the sit-in, but I tried to. I went to the building and told the people who were guarding the door that my boyfriend was in there, that he was the leader of this whole thing, and that I needed to see him right away. One of the student guards went inside and came back with Michael, who looked tired, fully absorbed, and remarkably sad. He took my hand and led me into the building. We sat on a bench some ways down from the biology lab turned war room, and he asked me if I could handle this.

"I'm okay. I can handle it," I said.

"Do you want to, though? Is this really you?" He had me there.

Now, Katherine, she could handle it. She sat the whole thing out, and in the end, she questioned where I was in the protest and the overall struggle. She knew I had white friends, and although she may have had a few herself, when push came to shove, she knew where she belonged, and she judged me harshly for choosing not to put myself in that same place.

When graduation came around a few months later, the seniors were asked to select a partner to walk with in the procession. I would have walked with Michael, but he was a year behind me. Katherine wanted me to walk with her, but I wanted to walk with my friend Larc, my white friend Larc. Katherine was surprised by my choice. "In the end," she said, "I mean, really, who do you think is going to be there for you? Do you think a white girl from Westport, Connecticut, is really going to have your back?"

I had been an easy target for Katherine throughout most of our friendship, and I could be made to feel very bad very quickly about not doing or being what I was supposed to do or be. But Larc was a good friend to me, and always had been. She called me out on my shit, backed me up when I felt alone in a room, was honest and generous with me about her own life and personal issues, made me laugh more than anyone I'd ever known, and never judged me. I told all this to Katherine, and she said, "Well then, you need to choose." And I did.

From my experience organizing the black student union at the University of New Hampshire, I understood that my political activism needed to come from a place that felt authentic to me, whether or not my position reflected that of the rest of the flock. This has been an ongoing lesson, and one that aspires to reflect Du Bois's wisdom, the third form born out of an imprisoned attitude: "a determined effort at self-realization and self-development despite environing opinion." The other two ways—"a feeling of revolt and revenge" and "an attempt to adjust all thought and action to the will of the greater group"—had not worked for me, had made me feel like a fraud.

While these words from the essay "Of Booker T. Washington and Others" are unambiguous, it is Kathleen Cleaver, the former Black Panther party member and ex-wife of Black Panther leader Eldridge Cleaver, who brought the concept home to me—the idea that there is another way to create revolution, even if it's as simple as claiming loyalty to a white friend.

Kathleen Cleaver

W. E. B. Du Bois outlined the options you have when you are enslaved, which are essentially revolt or submission. But once you have emancipation, then you have another option, and that is what he called "self-realization," or "self-development." Some people referred to these terms at the time they were used, as an indication of what later became Pan-Africanism or Black Nationalism. The point being: You don't have to respond to your oppressor; you can go down your own path.

Du Bois wrote about this notion of self-realization as

part of what he calls the history of the American Negro and the evolution of his successive leaders. The specific context was in his criticism of Booker T. Washington, which is very trenchant, but it's a broader idea as well, because he's analyzing how our struggle for emancipation, and against slavery, racism, and segregation, develops. I think about this in terms of the development of the Black Panther party, where you can see those elements that Du Bois pointed out—revolt, assimilation, and self-realization and self-determination.

I wouldn't say that nothing like the Black Panther party has happened over the past twenty years. I would say that the massive nature of the Black Panther party has been unparalleled. The Panther party was initially a very small group of people who came together in Oakland. At the same time, other small groups of black people in different cities across the country were also taking shape to deal with whatever the main issue they saw facing their city. On the West Coast, the key issue was police brutality. It wasn't until all these small clusters came together to form this powerful national wave that the Panther party took effect. The government was absolutely horrified. In the 1967 articulation of its counterintelligence program, it didn't even list the Black Panther party as an organization they wanted to get rid of. It listed the Nation of Islam, the Revolutionary Action Movement, the Student Nonviolent Coordinating Committee, and the Southern Christian Leadership Council. In 1968, the Black Panther party was their main focus.

So the way the Black Panther party and the move-ment around it exploded had a lot to do with other youth phenomena that were going on around the world at that time. To say that's not happening now—well, that partic-ular historical era is not happening now, that kind of mass movement is not happening now, but there are plenty of small groups today in different parts of the country that imitate and identify with the Black Panther party. They are not the same, not by any stripe of imagination, but they are out there trying to prompt change. There is that impetus. The circumstance in which these groups are op-erating is quite different, but the desire to make change is still present.

Right now, we're at a point of dissent—dissent about globalization, opposition to racism, opposition to forms of neocolonialism, opposition to war. It's not a progres-sive dissent, but it is still a form of dissent. And I have to have hope in that. What's the alternative? I could say, "Oh, I give up. The pigs have the right way. There is no alternative." But that's totally insane. The world that is being presented to us right now is a world based on geno-cide, ecocide, and homicide, that's unacceptable. To choose it is to choose your own destruction, and since I'm not self-destructive, I have to maintain hope in an al-ternative.

I don't see self-destruction in young black people as much as I see anger, but I also see a very enlightened group of people among today's black youth. I'm not going to say that they represent the majority, but then I also spend most of my time with people whose beliefs and human experiences are somewhat similar to mine. If I didn't, I'd probably feel very isolated and crushed. Maintaining hope and positive energy is a process that involves being with people who believe in particular ways of participating in the struggle. Du Bois is very central in that effort, because he was like that, as well—he was constantly on the case. What Du Bois wrote in 1903 about the slave trade and about Reconstruction is still viable. So it's not like we're whistling in the dark here.

In terms of figures from "black popular culture" or, as I refer to them, "the victims of commerce and racism," I see them on TV, I read about them in the papers, and I see what they do when they get the opportunity to express themselves culturally or politically. These are people who represent the triumph of a commercial, capitalist mindset. It's not that the people who are interested in transformation, reparations, social service in Africa, human rights, and protecting the environment are not out there, too; they just don't get the press. The popular media does not reflect what's going on in the country. The popular media reflects what the corporate owners of that media value.

And this goes back to the three trends outlined earlier—revolt, assimilation, or self-realization—because one of those three is always being emphasized or played out. The opposite of revolt is submission, and so what we are seeing now is submissive and assimilationist politics from anti–affirmative action types like the Ward Connerlys, or the Shelby Steeles. I grew up in the fifties. I heard people who thought like that all the time: "We're Americans; we're not Africans. This is the best we're gonna get." These are fairly conventional Negro voices of assimilation and submission, which, because they were not heard during the sixties and seventies, are being repositioned to be heard today. It's not that these voices didn't exist before. It's just that now they are saying things that the dominant Right prefers in terms of its political agenda. What we're looking at now in terms of politics is naked, rampant, predatory capitalism of the Enron variety. Under these circumstances, the centrally positioned black voices are going to be conservative.

There's a recording of a speech that Eldridge gave at Syracuse in 1968, and at the very beginning of the speech, he says that he heard me say, "You're either part of the problem or part of the solution." I had been quoting something I'd read, but he is the one who popularized that phrase, and it became identified with him. But it's just a slogan. It's not a belief structure. Many of the things that Eldridge said and his way of thinking in general presented an either/or situation. For example, one of the phrases that he used was, "Take your foot off my leg, motherfucker, or I'll blow your leg off," which is the same type of statement. It's an approach to dealing with reality.

The indoctrination that is out there is overwhelming,

and so people begin not to understand their own ability and power. My approach is: Let's clarify that you can make a difference. Let's clarify that you can rethink and transform how you view the world. Let's clarify that the world could be entirely different.

Chapter Nine

STRIVE AND STRIVE MIGHTILY

> . . . WHILE IT IS A GREAT TRUTH TO SAY THAT THE NEGRO
> MUST STRIVE AND STRIVE MIGHTILY TO HELP HIMSELF, IT
> IS EQUALLY TRUE THAT UNLESS HIS STRIVING BE NOT SIM-
> PLY SECONDED, BUT RATHER AROUSED AND ENCOURAGED,
> BY THE INITIATIVE OF THE RICHER AND WISER ENVIRONING
> GROUP, HE CANNOT HOPE FOR GREAT SUCCESS.
> —"Of Booker T. Washington and Others"

After I graduated from college in 1992, I moved to Boston, where I was told that my birth father, Jack Baynes—who was apparently known for hanging around the Berklee School of Music in the late 1960s and early 1970s—was last seen. I found an apartment on a street one block from the Berklee School and was hired as a research intern at Blackside Productions, the largest black-owned documentary film company in America, best known for its award-winning fourteen-part series *Eyes on the Prize*, which documented the civil rights movement.

I had learned of Blackside and *Eyes on the Prize* while in college, and I was excited about the opportunity of working with such a stalwart black organization. I was, though, far more focused on the possibility of bumping into my birth father. Even though I possessed only one picture of him, taken twenty-five years before—a profile shot of him wearing sunglasses, taken from a distance—I was sure that I would recognize him as soon as I saw him, and that I would magically match my eyes to his.

It wasn't as if I was in any kind of hurry to march into the Berklee School and ask the registrar or whomever if she knew of a guy named Jack Baynes who used to hang around there—the chance of seeing him one day somewhere on the street was too awesome to mess with. Plus, what if the registrar did know a guy named Jack Baynes? Then what?

The project I was hired to work on at Blackside was a documentary film for *The American Experience* series on PBS; it was called *Malcolm X: Make It Plain*. My unpaid internship included listening to taped speeches made by Malcolm X. Never in my life had I been so riveted, so moved, and so saddened by the loss of a human being as when I began listening to those tapes. Up until that point, all I'd known about Malcolm X was that he was angry, black, and had been shot dead. But here, I experienced the way his voice pulsated, the furor, the focus, the command of language, his courage, his dignity. I was absolutely turned out. I started to miss him terribly without ever having known him. I was not even alive when he was.

My birth mother (whose sole descriptive account of my birth father when we first met had been, "Basically, he was a dog") wanted nothing to do with any kind of encounter between us. She didn't actively discourage it, but she did make it resolutely clear that under no circumstances did she want him to know where she was or how to reach her. Fair enough—I respected that. Her brother, however, had maintained limited contact with him over the years, and he offered to set up a meeting on my behalf whenever I was ready. A few months after I moved to Boston, I was ready.

Jack Baynes didn't show up the first time. He did, however, show up the second time, with not so much of a fatherly embrace as a throttlehold of decaying desperation. He didn't seem to belong to anything or anyone. His dark skin glistened with sweat as tears gamboled loosely in his eyes as evidence of a cruel, unsatisfied longing endured for years. I asked him if he still played guitar, and he told me that he didn't because, he said, maybe he hadn't been good enough at it, or because he hadn't been inspired anymore after his baby girl—me—had been taken away from him by forces he could not control, because the white man, the government, didn't want him to win at anything. And, by the way, how was my mother? It had all been a conspiracy, he told me, that I had been taken away from him, just as slaves had been sold away from their families. If my mother hadn't been white—not that he didn't love her, because he did—none of this ever would have happened and we'd all still be together.

The next day at Blackside, as I listened to Malcolm's words, I thought of these two snuffed-out black men: Malcolm X and Jack Baynes—one immortalized, the other painfully mortal.

This account reflects, in some ways, Du Bois's cautionary suggestion that "while it is a great truth to say that the Negro must strive and strive mightily to help himself, it is equally true that unless his striving be not simply seconded, but rather aroused and encouraged, by the initiative of the richer and wiser environing group, he cannot hope for great success." Although perhaps arguable whether in "the richer and wiser environing group" Du Bois meant white America or those who have benefited from higher education, or both, for Malcolm X and my birth father, Jack Baynes, the "richer and wiser environing group" was indubitably white America. Malcolm only realized the positive value of said environing group's contribution and impact on his life and work shortly before his death—after a trip to Mecca, he returned with a newfound acceptance and appreciation of white people; months later, he was shot—while Jack Baynes, on the other hand, realized only the group's limitations.

For Vernon E. Jordan, who helped organize the integration of the University of Georgia and personally escorted Charlayne Hunter-Gault, one of the university's first black students, through a hostile white crowd in 1961, who has served as the Georgia field secretary for the National Association for the Advancement of Colored People (NAACP), as director of the

Voter Education Project for the Southern Regional Council, as head of the United Negro College Fund, as a delegate to President Lyndon B. Johnson's White House Conference on Civil Rights, as president and CEO of the National Urban League, and who has survived an assassination attempt, the "richer and wiser environing group" is Vernon E. Jordan himself.

Jordan has not so much sought out encouragement from white America, or the upper echelons of academe, as he has invited the option of what it, or they, may have to offer, an offer he may then accept or pass on. He has made discerning choices, and today, those choices, and the life and the man they have informed and helped to make, reveal not the secrets of a great success story. In fact, there are no secrets, no mystery, surrounding the extraordinary life of Vernon E. Jordan. He has, very simply, taken his life seriously, and he means for others to do the same.

Vernon E. Jordan, Jr.

i guess i've always pretty much known what I wanted to do and was determined to do it. I grew up in a house where there were no limitations put on my goals. I was encouraged by my parents to succeed, and although I knew that when I stepped outside of my home there would be this notion of a larger dominant group in the way of white America, I couldn't let that turn me around. People thought it was crazy that I wanted to be a lawyer, given the fact that black people could not go to law school in Georgia, or be in the bar association, for that matter. But that was not a deterrent as much as it was a reason to keep going. I have never believed that black people need the support of white people to succeed.

I invite the support of white people to the extent that I choose. All that I do and have done has always been my choice. When I got ready to go to college, the teachers at my high school in Georgia said, "Well, why are you going up there? Morehouse isn't good enough for you?" They didn't understand why I wanted to leave the South to go to college. And I said, "Because I want to." I had some notion that if I stayed down south and went to Morehouse that today I would still be hanging on the corner of Thayer and Chestnut, watching the girls go by. I was interested in the bigger challenge, the larger world, and I wanted to grow in ways that I thought I would not have grown if I had stayed in Georgia.

On August 15, 1953, my mother left a note on my bed that said, "We want you to go to college wherever you want to go. If you go to Howard, you might be more comfortable, more at home academically and socially. But you go wherever you want to go." And that's what I did. I lost my buddies, though. We had decided that we were all going to Howard together—we were going to rent a house, have a car, be sharp every day and chase good-looking women. That was the plan. But then this guy came to my high school from the National Service of Scholarship Funds for Negro Students, and he talked about the option of going to school up north—and I got interested in the idea. I applied to Dartmouth and Depauw University in Greencastle, Indiana, where I was accepted. After that, one night when I had to work, my girlfriend went out with my buddies, and I became the topic of conversation. They said things like, "He thinks he's white; he thinks he's smarter than us." The next night, my girlfriend told me, "Your friends are not your friends. They think you're breaking rank." And then she told me to go on up there to college in Indiana anyway and do what I had to do.

There was nothing in my mind telling me I needed to go to a white school to succeed—I wasn't mature enough to think about it as a strategy. It was just what I wanted to do. Right after I finished high school, I went up to Depauw for an educational guidance conference, and I was the only black among about fifty students. The director of admissions told me that Depauw was not the school for me, and that I should go to Ball State. He also told me that the notion of my wanting to be a lawyer was crazy, and that I'd probably end up being a high school social science teacher. I just said to him, "I'll be back."

While my parents were proud of my decision, there was some trepidation on their part because I was going into what they thought could be a hostile environment. They took me to school. We drove—my parents, my brother, and I—to Greencastle, and they all spent the weekend there with me. We went to mixers and met various professors at the university, as well as important figures from town, like the bank president—it's a very warm town. The last night, my brother shook my hand and ran off, all excited that he'd have the bedroom to himself for the first time; my mother, with tears running down her face, kissed me and said, "God bless you, son"; my daddy told me I couldn't "come home." He said, "These teachers think these kids are smarter than you. They read faster. They went to better schools than you. But you can't come home." I was stunned by that, and I asked him, "What am I supposed to do then, Daddy?" And he said, "Read, boy, read." When I graduated four years later, he came up to me, shook my hand, and told me I could come home.

I didn't go to Depauw University just to learn. By my very presence there, I was a teacher, as well. And that didn't bother me, because my view was that whatever problem the white students might have with me was not mine, but theirs. I don't know where that conviction came from, but I knew that if I allowed myself to be uncomfortable in their presence, I was doomed. That has been my attitude about everything. When I was growing up and we went downtown to segregated Atlanta, my mother would say before we left, "Go to the bathroom now. Drink your water now. So that when we get downtown, you don't have to subject yourself to the system." So we peed before we went downtown.

There's a passage in the introduction to my book (*Vernon Can Read!*) that reads: "I choose to stick with what I know and believe fervently about the progress of black life during the decades of which I write." The way I feed that belief is just by living it—get up every morning, go to work, work hard, take nothing for granted. I believe that whatever I want, I need to get for myself. There are no handouts, and I don't want them anyway. I just want to go to work every day. I want the same opportunities these other guys, white guys, get. The thing I know for sure is that the Man will take care of himself—the white man. It's my job to work it out so that I can be where he is on an equal basis, because if I am, he cannot take care of himself without equally taking care of me. I think that's what it's all about. Does it work the other way—if I'm taking care of myself, am I equally taking care of the white man? I don't worry about him, because he's always going to be all right. I worry about the brothers and sisters, though, because the support system is different for them.

This notion of a support system is relevant to what Du Bois was talking about in *The Souls of Black Folk* in terms of an "environing group." When I went to college, the only thing my daddy could give me was permission. That was not true of any of the white boys I went to school with, but I could not worry about that. Being born into Phillips Exeter Academy was their garden to tend, not mine. I needed to tend my own garden.

I don't mention Du Bois in my book. But if you look through my speeches over time, starting at the Urban League, I quoted him a lot. I read *The Souls of Black Folk* for the first time simultaneously with *Up from Slavery*, by Booker T. Washington, while I was in college. Even though I thought they were both right, I especially loved what Du Bois said about the responsibility of the Talented Tenth to the masses. Du Bois thought, and he was right about this, that we had to have a cadre of educated people to lead, to plan, and to teach. I believed it then, I believe it now, and that is how I've tried to live my life.

My view of the Du Bois–Washington debate is that like most things in life, it was not either/or; it was both/and. An example of that is if you go to Atlanta today: The jobs that we used to dominate—as electricians, waiters, doormen, tailors, and barbers—in part because of the Talented Tenth theory, we don't dominate anymore. Du Bois was right about the responsibility of the educated, but everybody can't go to Morehouse, and we need to figure out something for those folks to do. And Washington said, "Teach them farming, tooling, and so forth."

There is a direct relationship between the farmers and the cadre of leaders. They have one commonality—their blackness. When the white man discriminated, he didn't make a choice between the educated and the uneducated black man. It was "To Whom It May Concern" if you were black, and to a certain extent, it still is. I can stand next to an elevator porter on Sixth Avenue in New York dressed in my suit and my Turnbull shirt, and neither one of us will get a taxi.

Du Bois was quite uppity. When he lived in Atlanta, you'd see him around town in his black suits and his spats. He was not a man of the people. John Hope Franklin (the great civil rights leader and historian, and author of the classic book *From Slavery to Freedom: A History of African Americans*) tells a great story about Du Bois, and he can tell it much better than I can, but I'll do my best. When John Hope Franklin was a student at Harvard, he worked in Durham, North Carolina, during the summers. If you were traveling between Washington and Atlanta, Durham was one of the few places where you could stop and there would be black restaurants. John Hope Franklin was a waiter at one of these restaurants, and Du Bois came in one day, alone, and Franklin was very excited to see him. He went over to Du Bois and said, "My name is John Hope Franklin. Like you, I went to Fisk University." Du Bois said nothing. Franklin said, "I'm also a student of history at Harvard, like you." Du Bois said nothing. Franklin said, "I'm also going to get a Ph.D. from Harvard, as you did." And finally, Du Bois said, "Good evening." He was not a man of the people.

The great contradiction about Du Bois is that even as he was not a man of the people, he could write truthfully and eloquently about the people. For that, he is forgiven. He understood the aspirations of black people, and that understanding lives on.

Chapter Ten

THE QUESTION OF THE FUTURE

> I INSIST THAT THE QUESTION OF THE FUTURE IS HOW
> BEST TO KEEP THESE MILLIONS FROM BROODING OVER THE
> WRONGS OF THE PAST AND THE DIFFICULTIES OF THE
> PRESENT, SO THAT ALL THEIR ENERGIES MAY BE BENT TO-
> WARD A CHEERFUL STRIVING AND CO-OPERATION WITH
> THEIR WHITE NEIGHBORS TOWARD A LARGER, JUSTER, AND
> FULLER FUTURE.
>
> —"Of the Training of Black Men"

For one year, I was the face of first defense at the Afro-American Studies Department at Harvard University. I answered phones, greeted students, professors, and guest lecturers, filed papers and evaluations, and sorted mail for the entire department. During my time there, I met and became good friends with an undergraduate student named Karen. With chocolate-colored skin and beautiful, shiny, bold eyes, Karen was always giving me trouble over my fashion sense: "Sweetie, I know you were raised by white people, but girl, those boots with that skirt?" She would tell me that I looked like some mixed, bohemian, free-loving black girl from the cast of *A Different World*, which was fine if that's what I was going for, but "Dear God, girl," she would say, "you know you need to put some oil in that hair."

Also while a receptionist at the Afro-American Studies Department, I met and briefly dated a graduate student named Tom. Tom had green eyes, dark brown hair, and broad, gallant shoulders. He was completely white-looking. In fact, I assumed he was white—lots of white students were Afro-American Studies majors—until we started talking more, and he told me that his father, who had died when Tom was a child, was black, and that Tom also considered himself black. The more I got to know him, the more fascinated I became by this identity he had created for himself partly, it seemed, out of respect and reverence for and in memory of his father, and partly because he genuinely felt akin to a black cultural sensibility.

Karen was skeptical about him from the get-go. She thought he was too slick, too handsome, and spent too much damn time in the Afro-American Studies Department. One afternoon when Karen and I were chatting at my desk, Tom came through on his way to a class.

"I don't trust him," Karen said when he was safely out of earshot.

"Oh, come on. He's smart and he's fine. You know he is," I argued.

"Yeah, girl, but you know what he *isn't*."

In Karen's view, Tom could claim blackness all he wanted, and his father's, too, for that matter, but that still wouldn't make him black. The criteria was tacitly understood between us—tacitly understood, largely because it had first been tacitly imposed by most, if not all, of white America. There is something so acutely rational about this line of thinking. Why bother with the confusion of cultural idiosyncrasies when the skin color is right there like a tribal mark, a war scar. Seems it could be, and maybe should be, that simple.

Karen was protective about someone assuming an identity she felt she herself had hard-learned, but to what detriment? What was she missing by sustaining this limited perspective, and what was I missing by agreeing, even as I continued to grapple with my own "authenticity"? Would our harsh expectations lessen and our seemingly finite definitions broaden if we allowed for and encouraged an aesthetically different-looking "blackness" to exist in the future? The latter, indeed, is what Du Bois implied in the following statement from "Of the Training of Black Men": "I insist that the question of the future is how best to keep these millions from brooding over the wrongs of the past and the difficulties of the present, so that all their energies may be bent toward a cheerful striving and co-operation with their white neighbors toward a larger, juster, and fuller future."

Former New Jersey councilman Cory Booker, a light-skinned African American man who ran for mayor of Newark, New Jersey, in 2001 and who suffered repeated attacks suggesting that he was not "black enough," has made the question of how best to keep the millions from brooding his main platform as a community leader and activist. And, like Du Bois, Booker believes that the answer to this question, so long overdue, will reveal itself in voices louder and less parochial than those we have heard thus far.

Cory Booker

i grew up with parents who were deeply rooted in where they came from, and so I had the sense growing up that I was the manifestation of that sense of rootedness. For me, the way to best honor that, and what I've always known I wanted to do, is to be part of the struggle, part of the fight. And I believe that we need everyone in order to fight that fight effectively.

There's a great Du Bois quote in which he says, and I'm paraphrasing, "In a world where it means so much to take a man by the hand and sit beside him, to look frankly into his eyes and feel his heart beating with red blood, one can imagine the consequences of the absence of social amenities between estranged races, whose separation extends even to parks and streetcars." In my work, a lot of what I do is about getting people to move beyond the separation.

During the mayoral campaign, there were many things that were said, targeting my racial identity and allegiance, including the suggestion that I first needed to learn how to be an African American before I could be the mayor of Newark. For someone to question my background, especially when you look at someone like Du Bois, who was such a scholar, and to suggest that I'm not black enough based on whatever reasons is absurd. But there have always been black Americans who have been criticized by other black Americans for being what the latter might call "sellouts"—people who have won or sought the approval of the so-called mainstream, like Althea Gibson, Bayard Rustin, Ralph Bunche, even Sidney Poitier. I don't especially mind the criticism, as long as I'm being true to myself, and in my heart know what I'm trying to do.

It's always disheartening when black people turn against one another. It was disturbing to me, for example, when I heard Harry Belafonte's recent criticism of Colin Powell, which was based solely on some sort of racial protocol. [In an October 2002 interview with talk show host Ted Leitner on the San Diego radio station KFMB-AM, Belafonte was quoted as saying, "There's an old saying in the days of slavery. There are those slaves who lived on the plantation, and there were those who lived in the house. You got the privilege of living in the house if you served the master. Colin Powell was permitted to come into the house of the master."] Belafonte could tear Colin Powell apart for some of his political beliefs, and I might join him in that criticism, but who is Harry Belafonte, as great as he is, to be a purveyor of blackness with regard to select individuals? To call somebody out for not being black enough—there's just no time for that. We, as in the social fabric of America, have so many other issues to contend with.

I resist any notions that there is one way to be black, and I have defined myself and my life with that in mind, and as something that will evolve as I continue to grow and learn. What my "blackness" means to me—the blood quotient, the color of my skin—is an evolving, dynamic process. My grandfather, for example, who had a black mother and a white father, although he was not raised by his father, has had an extraordinary "black experience" in his lifetime. His trials, challenges, and his struggles growing up in Louisiana constitute a great "black" story. The fabric is threaded deep. So to say that there is some sort of hegemonic African American experience is to discount so many individual experiences we've all had.

Each black person has his or her own individual yearning; it is one that is and should be part of an important ideal for black culture, because this is a collective struggle, but it is also important in the struggle waged by humanity in general. I think it was Henry Louis Gates who said that he luxuriates in his blackness, but that in the end, his blackness is merely a portal into a deeper understanding of humanity. I agree, and so one of the gifts that my skin color allows for is a better appreciation of the texture of humanity and a deeper ability to feel compassion.

Celebrating and luxuriating in my blackness and gaining access to that portal, not only helps me to feel a powerful bond with other black people, other people of color, but also with humanity as a whole, people who have had different experiences than I have. My understanding of self allows me access to others, and what I think is most important is for us all to strive toward a sort of social justice where we create a sense of kinship with others who have had both similar and not so similar experiences.

One powerful aspect of this country as a whole is that when people strike out to be different, although they are often criticized in the beginning, they also often become some of our greatest leaders, because of the courage it took in order to beat their own drum. As the eighteenth-century English poet Edward Young said, "We're all born originals—why is it that so many of us die copies?" It's the original people, the ones who are not only original but also thinking originally, the ones who dare to imagine—those are the people we should look to and aspire toward.

I have no patience for people who exploit racial fear

or insecurity for their own gain. And, frankly, I have no patience for people who try to foster their own sense of security by being part of a group and pushing a point of false solidarity. You know, I struggle in my own life with trying not to be concerned with what other people think—we all do—and when I meet or see people who have views that I find are so limiting not just to the black community but to the larger human community, I try to remember that while I may be able to do nothing about their feelings or ideas, I can live my life in a way that is whole.

Can it be a lonely path? Of course. But I think everybody feels lonely at one point or another. And, too, I think there's an isolation that comes with being politically active. It's easy to forget the ten compliments or expressions of appreciation that you might get on any given day, and then to go to sleep that night thinking only about the negative things you've heard. But that's a very self-absorbed way to live your life.

My father used to say that there are two ways that you can go through life: as a thermometer or as a thermostat—someone, like a thermometer, who allows himself to be affected by the temperature of the environment, or someone, like a thermostat, who actually sets the temperature of the environment. I also try to remember the connection I have to a higher power. I'm a Christian, but I have a very broad conception of what that higher power is. Mainly, I think of it as an abundant and amazing source of energy and consciousness that connects us all in ways that we're not even aware of, and I'm happy to be part of any mission with the goal of expanding that connection.

I think that while this generation may not necessarily be able to redefine what race means to us, we can at least see it as an evolving definition. I hope my children and the children of this generation have a different experience and outlook on race than we do and that those before us did. I'm a prisoner of hope, of change, and of optimism. The active belief in change is what makes it probable, and so I have no plans of giving up.

Chapter Eleven

FRANK AND FAIR

> It is, then, the strife of all honorable men of the twentieth century to see that in the future competition of races the survival of the fittest shall mean the triumph of the good, the beautiful, and the true. . . . To bring this hope to fruition, we are compelled daily to turn more and more to a conscientious study of the phenomena of race-contact,—to a study frank and fair, and not falsified and colored by our wishes or our fears.
>
> —"Of the Sons of Master and Man"

As a first-time history teacher with no professional training, the only way I knew how to teach the eleventh-grade students at a small private school for girls in the suburbs of Boston was by being honest. It was the 1995–1996 academic year, when the Million Man March, the O. J. Simpson trial, and ethnic cleansing in Bosnia unfolded in the news like a culturally explicit, race-charged trilogy of historical nonfiction—ripe material for a twenty-five-year-old with high and righteous ideals, who also happened to be the only black woman on the faculty.

In addition to a junior-year history class, I also taught a freshman English class. With a degree and background in writing and literature, the latter was easier, but the former was more satisfying. The kids were largely from moneyed families, and all but a fistful were white. I was young enough to identify with their popular interests, old enough to command authority, and hip enough to appeal to their sensibilities. We learned history in a backward glance, starting from the day at hand, which meant that I asked them to write papers on the Million Man March, let them watch live coverage of the O.J. trial, and spent a considerable amount of time making sure they understood that the concept of ethnic cleansing was not intrinsic to Bosnia.

Perhaps unlike other teachers of high school American history (certainly all of mine anyway), I didn't teach the subjects of race and slavery in one condensed section—slaves, not slaves, Jim Crow, Reconstruction, and so forth. I taught slave history and race as a social construct that has evolved and viciously asserted itself at several different and important junctures over the past century, not least of all during the formation of contemporary social politics. The girls grew to appreciate my open, fairly progressive, and unique (to them) style of teaching, and they grew to trust me. It wasn't until about midyear, when I asked my students to explain the meaning of racism within the context of what we had learned in class thus far, that they began to get nervous.

"What is racism?" I asked the class. Normally a very animated, outspoken, and participatory group, the girls fell silent. I knew I had to be careful, but I also knew that I wasn't going to get them to think unless I was pointed and unflinching.

"Jane," I said, calling on one of my less academically and more conversationally inclined students. "Are you a racist?"

Jane looked at me as though I were introducing a new line of soccer cleat, not quite sure she wanted to buy it but, as a star soccer player, knowing she at least needed to consider the product's viability.

"Um, no," she said with appropriate hesitation, all the while looking me straight in the eye.

"Then don't sweat it."

Jane smiled slowly, then laughed uncomfortably, and, finally, went on to tell me and the rest of the class why she gave the answer she did, why she didn't think she could ever be a racist, and why understanding racism and the dynamic between black and white Americans was so important to her, and to society at large.

Jane was brave. I was brave. That's how it's done.

In his essay "Of the Sons of Master and Man," Du Bois talks about striving toward a sense of moral fairness for the future—"the strife of all honorable men of the twentieth century to see that in the future competition of races the survival of the fittest shall mean the triumph of the good"—and by "honorable men," he meant honorable people (as the word *men* was interchangeable with the word *humanity* in 1903). Du Bois goes on to suggest that one of the ways by which to achieve such a victory is through means of "a study frank and fair." No smoke and mirrors, no cushioning the blow, keeping the conversation interesting, but also keeping it real, as we might say today.

In her efforts toward fostering racial and gender equality, Jewell Jackson McCabe, founder and president of the National Coalition of 100 Black Women, is among those who have kept it real. Quoted in the 1989 photography book *I Dream a World: Portraits of Black Women Who Changed America*, McCabe offered up this simple apothegm as a means of shooting straight amid the ongoing navigation of race relations: "You factor in racism as reality, and you keep moving." It doesn't get more frank and fair than that.

Jewell Jackson McCabe

The contradiction that Du Bois or any complex intellectual faces in being prophetic and interpreting oppression is saying one thing and sometimes living another. Not long after *The Souls of Black Folk* was published, Du Bois wrote a particularly profound essay called "The Damnation of Black Women." For a man of his century to have had such keen and clear and impassioned feelings about pro-feminism is really quite extraordinary, and I would suggest it was because of the women who surrounded him in his life, both personally and professionally.

Du Bois was adamant about the portrayal of black womanhood, and the treatment of black women. He tried to shun or step away from the contemporary images of beauty, which were cast in the mold of Europeans. Yet, in his actual life, he was very much drawn to and equally compelled to be with women who had what would be considered stereotypically beautiful characteristics. So I think the complexity for Du Bois as a race-conscious, feminist-conscious male leader, the conundrum was that his social politics were not reflected in his personal life. As harsh as that reality maybe—he is still heroic—he analyzed, he critiqued, and, most important, he committed to paper his accounts of early-twentieth-century white misogynistic patriarchy and its practices against the "Negro" woman under siege: the naked hatred, the degradation, the misinterpretation, the cruel treatment, and, as he worded it, "the unendurable paradox of black women." This is the experience of African American women then and now.

I would speculate that if one is trained in the European form—Elizabethan English, history, and culture—as the scholar and intellectual Du Bois was, one has a disciplined sense of self and a thirst for analytical exploration and critical thinking. If imbued with both Eurocentric sensibility and Afrocentric pride, one faces the conundrum that underscores the Du Bois contradiction. This ambiguous position with regard to a system of values has not changed for most African Americans over the course of the last one hundred years. This is why Du Bois was most profound in saying that "the problem of the twentieth century is the problem of the color-line." Here we are in the twenty-first century, with no generational plan for the cultural equity and creation of wealth that we are committed to. Even though in Washington, D.C., the Reverend Martin Luther King, Jr., laid out a blueprint on August 28, 1963, it is as if we are partially deaf and unwilling to comprehend. We only seem to remember or have heard that he had a dream. Shame on us—still no answer or organized means toward achieving social change.

In some respect, we are agents and purveyors of our own degrading messages and images. Anytime our rap artists and producers refer to African American women as their "gangsta bitches," I would suggest we have astonishing confusion within the race, in addition to what we are projecting to the mainstream community at large. And this is only one example of the mixed signals we allow our children to grapple with under the guise of participating in the system of market-driven free enterprise.

It is still extraordinarily difficult for people to trust and communicate with one another. Psychologists, behavioral scientists, and communication experts have analyzed and broken down verbal communication into three components: language, or the spoken word: 7 percent; attitude: 38 percent; and chemistry: 55 percent. So, while the vocabulary we use is both significant and essential in negotiating race relations—or anything else, for that matter—we communicate primarily through our attitude and our chemistry. However, I would say that by managing attitude, you may affect chemistry. When we experience charisma, we are usually mesmerized by attitude and seduced by the chemistry of "the leader." Sadly, we have so few charismatic leaders today. However, I am a believer that we come from a strong line with a legacy of greatness and that the pendulum will swing back and we will once again find our voice of moral authority. For now, we have to play the hand we've been dealt, and not allow ourselves to get distracted by the inevitability of classism, racism, and sexism.

Du Bois, along with the great thinker, journalist, and activist Ida B. Wells and educator Anna Julia Cooper offers the ultimate example of our intellectual prowess as black people connected to a historic legacy. It's important to recognize that, because most people, depending upon their generation and geography, have not a clue about our legacy. We must provide historic memory. The reason is simple; it's not rocket science. With few exceptions, we have a broken and bankrupt educational system at every level. We still live in a country with a patriarchal system.

It wasn't until the early twentieth century that women got the right to vote, and we still have not been recognized in the Constitution by the passage of the Equal Rights Amendment. Technology in the twenty-first century has created the digital divide in America's continuing schizoid class war. Education, ideology, and wealth are the essential elements for progressive social change. I often say that the least accomplished African American male would be considered a candidate to lead a major African American organization before the most accomplished intellectually expansive, qualified, resourceful African American woman. And yet black women are allowed to lead their own groups to advise presidents, and to lead mainstream institutions.

Take, for example, Ruth Simmons, president of Brown University, the first African American to lead an Ivy League school; Marion Wright Edelman, who founded and heads the Children's Defense Fund, the premier advocacy group for this country's more than 60 million children; and Condoleezza Rice, national security adviser to the president of the United States. There is also, of course, Faye Wattleton, who led Planned Parenthood during the turbulent times when the Supreme Court was debating over a woman's right to choose.

But entrenched sexism and the psychological scar of slavery have resulted in the black community denying itself the benefit of 60 percent of its gray matter by failing to recognize black women as leaders. What's up with that? And so for a patriarchal system to allow for greater recognition of a figure like Du Bois seems far off the mark, at best.

This is a cynical statement, but it is sort of gratifying to watch Jay Leno when he does his "people on the street" segment, "Jay Walking," where he stops all types of average Americans, including white elementary schoolteachers who, when shown a photograph of George W. Bush, can't identify the president of the United States. Yes, there is a dearth of knowledge about current and past events and lack of historical context for the American dream. Significantly, people hear what they want to hear about a racist, classist, sexist society. If you're saying things that are progressive or perhaps edgy and your vision challenges the status quo, most people are going to reject what you have to say, because they prefer to be in denial, anesthetized by sameness.

One of the realities of a capitalist society—which I endorse, by the way—is that we need to ensure progressive, standardized, intergenerational, multicultural education that allows for gender equity and that chronicles a synergistic history. Currently, this system keeps dumbing down and balkanizing. Take, for example, stereotypic programming for television, with its five hundred–plus channels and all its superstations. The lack of cultural and educational synergy, especially for people who are economically disadvantaged, portends a bleak future. If all the images you have of black people come essentially from Black Entertainment Television (BET), we are in big trouble, and the ancestors are weeping in their graves.

The fact that you can read Du Bois today and it is as contemporary as it was in 1903 should make us rise up and take stock of our role. It shows us that we must be ever vigilant. There are those who have to continue providing breakthrough leadership, those who have to continue monitoring the breakthrough, and then those who have to be relentless and continue reinventing the wheel. How do we change this? Through books like this one and through organizations like mine that commit ideas to print and speak up. As I've often said, in my leadership I want to be able to make my agenda, equity—bringing the voice of women of color to the table—a part of the total portfolio of the people.

We African Americans came to these shores in 1619, deemed chattel by the Founding Fathers in the Constitution, defined as three-fifths human, and condemned to statutory punishment by death if educated or taught to read. In 1863, the Emancipation Proclamation gave so-called freedom. Yet we lived under a rule of law that sanctioned separate and "unequal" treatment until *Plessy v. Ferguson* was overturned in 1954 by the Supreme Court's *Brown v. Topeka Board of Education* decision, which legally put an end to the demeaning, destructive, psychological lynching known as "Jim Crow." It would be yet another decade before the proverbial playing field was leveled by the "children" of the South. We got the Civil Rights Act in 1964 and the potent Voting Rights Act in 1965, and during that amazing period we saw a new day dawn in America. We elected a governor, we revisited the Senate, and we elected black mayors to rural cities and thriving urban centers. And let us not forget the historic election of Ron Brown to chair the Democratic National Committee.

Since the sixties, we have seen two generations that

have grown up benefiting from the hard-earned victories of the modern day civil rights movement. Today, we do have a few extraordinary entrepreneurs, and captains of industry running Fortune 100 companies. We have made quantum leaps, yet mainstream images of our people are horrific—in some cases more insulting and as damaging as that of "Amos 'n' Andy," which the NAACP fought to remove from the airwaves. That's a fact.

To motivate our children and "generations yet to come," we need to promote images of success that mirror the total spectrum of our involvement in every discipline in American society. We need to go back to using role models. Every other ethnic segment of American society is judged by its highest level of achievement. Most disturbing, African Americans are characterized by a monolithic block of ignorant stereotypic caricatures. And dangerously, if our youth excel, set high standards of excellence in terms of traditional education, they are often ridiculed by their own as "acting white."

In many ways, we have reinvented Jim Crow and are enslaving ourselves. The question of how to solve this problem is both simple and complex. America is driven by capitalism, and black people were thwarted from the creation of wealth for over three centuries. It is only in the last generation that we have seen Oprah Winfrey, CEO, Harpo Productions; Stanley O'Neal, CEO, Merrill Lynch; Ken Chenault, CEO, American Express; Dick Parsons, CEO, AOL Time Warner; Ann Fudge, CEO, Young &

Rubicam. These figures are among the first African Americans to earn salaries commensurate with their white counterparts.

We are just now coming into a new kind of leadership, and that is the answer to the question. We must be smart and exploit these breakthroughs for what they are, create a "back bench" for continuity, and ensure that we, too, are judged by our highest level of achievement. It is a wonderful and thoughtful question, but the question presupposes that people will wake up early and go to bed late in pursuit of excellence, proceeding with unrelenting determination, knowing the ancestors are watching as we do our part in immortalizing the legacy. Let's *keep it* real, frank, and *make it* fair.

Chapter Twelve

THE RULE OF INEQUALITY

> . . . THE RULE OF INEQUALITY: THAT OF THE MILLION
> BLACK YOUTH, SOME WERE FITTED TO KNOW AND SOME
> TO DIG; THAT SOME HAD THE TALENT AND CAPACITY OF
> UNIVERSITY MEN, AND SOME THE TALENT AND CAPACITY
> OF BLACKSMITHS; AND THAT TRUE TRAINING MEANT NEI-
> THER THAT ALL SHOULD BE COLLEGE MEN NOR ALL ARTI-
> SANS . . .
>
> —"Of the Wings of Atalanta"

After the publication of my second book, I was awarded a grant
from the W. K. Kellogg Foundation and appointed by Henry
Louis Gates, Jr., as a fellow at the W. E. B. Du Bois Institute at
Harvard University, where I was given an office in which to
work and conduct research for my next book—a collection of

interviews with young black girls in America. It was a very exciting opportunity and, I might add, deliciously satisfying to have been a receptionist at Harvard's Afro-American Studies Department the year before and then, at twenty-six, to be listed with the likes of Cornel West, William Julius Wilson, Evelyn Brooks Higginbotham, and Kwame Anthony Appiah on the institute's colloquia roster. It was not that I considered myself an intellectual peer of these obviously brilliant and far more advanced scholars, although I did feel worthy of my appointment and confident about my contribution to the institute.

I had just ended a year of teaching at a small private school outside of Boston, and I was juggling various jobs, as I often had throughout my life when I hit a financial wall. The grant money had run out, and I suddenly found myself in a situation where I had no money coming in at all, and nothing lined up to generate any kind of income. I've never been very good at saving or managing money, although I have always been willing to work exceedingly hard at making it.

During the months of my appointment, I had become friendly with a professor affiliated with the Institute, and I decided to write him a letter expressing my financial concerns. Soon after, I received a call from his secretary, who asked if I might like to pack boxes at his house for ten dollars an hour. He was in the process of moving and thought I might appreciate the opportunity to make a few bucks.

I was humiliated, and my pride deeply wounded. I wrote him another letter, in which I stated that no, thank you, I would not like to pack boxes for ten dollars an hour. I also told him, with the righteous indignation of a young woman scorned, that the offer itself reeked of antebellum condescension. He called me himself this time. "Look," he said, with short, chunky, disconnected strands of regret, reprimand, and compassion, "I was just trying to help you."

Certainly, I wish the whole exchange had never happened, and I do believe he meant well, but at the time, the situation did evoke in me the sense that some, particularly within the hedged confines of academe, were suited to pack boxes and some to have their boxes packed, just as Du Bois assesses of black youth, within a comparable context, in the essay "Of the Wings of Atalanta," when he avers that "some were fitted to know and some to dig." Spoken from a place of both elitism and realism, even as the importance and restorative measure of education never falls far from nearly every point made in *Souls*, Du Bois accepted that not everyone would be up to the task. Du Bois then reveals in a somewhat surreptitiously witty remark what appears to be more tolerance than acceptance of this fact: "to seek to make the blacksmith a scholar is almost as silly as the more modern scheme of making the scholar a blacksmith; almost, but not quite."

But what happens when a tolerance, an understanding of sorts, like this is cultivated not as a luxury of human limitation but as a mirror image of the preemptive social archetype? And why does Du Bois refer to this notion of apparent natural selection as "the rule of inequality"?

Inherent in the well-known 1990 protest made by former

Harvard law professor and author Derrick Bell, who is now on the faculty at New York University, against Harvard University's hiring policies, with specific charges against the university for having never hired a black woman for tenure, is the suggestion that Harvard, which also happens to be the alma mater of W. E. B. Du Bois, stands among the academic orders in modern history that not only uphold the theory that some are fit to know and some to dig but executes it with arbitrary force. Perhaps, then, the question is not who is fit to know but, rather, who decides who is fit to know.

Derrick Bell

i am increasingly suspicious of words like *equality* and *inequality*—like *racism* or *racist*, these words have lost all direct, insightful meaning. What we are talking about here, in this particular Du Bois quote and in Rebecca Carroll's remarks above is, rather, the rule of racial presumption. Starting off with the above remarks, I wondered if I had gotten this letter, expressing these desperate straits, and I had research to be done, if not very exciting research, perhaps checking citations, would I have offered that job? Perhaps it is different, citing research and packing boxes.

The situation does bring to mind that for folk who are always presumed to be less than at least they consider themselves to be, survival is key. Now, it would have been different if that professor had said, "I am packing boxes, and I would love to talk with you about such and such, and we could pack boxes together, and I could pay you ten dollars an hour." It's the status and munitions that were disconcerting.

Then, though, I also thought of the ongoing struggle at virtually every major mainly white university to get hired those people of color with promise, as we would measure it. But because they do not have the kind of credentials that many of their white counterparts do, they are considered undesirable hires—unless there is some dire situation and a position absolutely needs to be filled. As my late wife, Jewel, once put it when we were coming from a fancy dinner at the home of a colleague, "Your colleagues are smart, but many of them are not impressive." She just nailed it, and that was a great help to me, because race was a factor but so, too, were their backgrounds. They had all gone to major schools—I didn't go to a major school; they had all clerked at the Supreme Court—I didn't clerk at anybody's court. They didn't treat me poorly, but it was clear that there was a gap.

Many times, the few people of color who share the same credentials as their white colleagues, and who are very often sought after, fall into the same groove as those white colleagues: They are writing the great piece, which almost never gets written, and, sadly, they are not good teachers. They are like—and this is not my quote—the priests who have lost their faith and kept their jobs. It is a great frustration, but it seems to me that this is what the Du Bois quote here speaks to—that people should not be labeled because of their backgrounds, and that there may well be some who are fitted to know and some to dig, but to assume that based on where someone grew up, where they went to school, and what color they are is to make a gigantic error.

I think that we lose at whatever point we choose to make such an assumption, because it harms both those who make it and those who are victimized by the making. To assume that blacks who went to Harvard, have served on the *Law Review,* and clerked on the Supreme Court are going to be great scholars and teachers can be as wrong as the assumption that someone who is a janitor can only clean up after others.

Very few black folk are able to get totally beyond presumption of incompetence. The fact is that those who are even modestly welcome in certain academic circles are the most welcomed they will ever be. Once you start standing up, though, and saying, "I'm not here to kiss your behind," then there are problems. I don't think that anybody escapes, and those black folk who claim that they have escaped are probably more damaged than they know. There is, perhaps, individual change on the horizon, and it is certainly a different world from the one in which Du Bois lived: No school or university is officially saying to black folk, "Don't even try to get this job, or this training," but once you enter that school or university, and if you have any kind of sensitivity at all, you very quickly understand that you are expected to have a mediocre career at best.

I don't think that Du Bois had low expectations of black folk. I think he was merely issuing a warning that there are millions of folk who may or may not be suitable college men, but that true training would provide opportunities in either direction. So we wouldn't track kids in grade one; in fact, we probably wouldn't track kids at all. In his great statement of 1933 on the integrated versus segregated school situation, he acknowledged that integrated schools might be better and that many segregated schools were bad, but, he said, all things being equal, black children need neither integrated nor segregated schools; what they need is education.

It is a simple and profound statement, but, like so many of the things that Du Bois said, it was ignored. Du Bois was probably the most brilliant man of his time, and the most ignored man of his time, because often the things that he said or wrote did not fall within the rather narrow ambit of what everyone else was thinking. And that also happens today with things said by black folk— the more simple and profound, the more likely to go unnoticed. I'm not sure we can change that, or prevent that from happening, because the factors that lead to it are so ingrained. Our obligation is to know that and, in our own way, not to allow that to keep us from speaking the truth. Our obligation is not to change the world but to recognize its evils and to work at what we can do.

Yes, it is a different world from the one when Du Bois was living. I don't think you can ignore the fact that black folk are in job, housing, and school situations that would have seemed impossible in Du Bois's time. The problem is that there are official and unofficial limits to how many black folks will be allowed into any one of those situations.

In one of my fictional Geneva Crenshaw stories, she's teaching at a law school and is about ready to quit because there are so few black faculty there, until this strange guy comes out of nowhere and tells her that he understands her problems and that he can produce black faculty for her. He does, and the black faculty goes from one, Geneva, to six. Then he produces this truly outstanding man, and the dean says to Geneva, "I think we should send him to our sister school across town." And Geneva says, "I'm not recruiting for our sister school; this man is great." And the dean says, "Yeah, but, you know, that will make seven black members of our faculty; a quarter of our faculty will be black. You have to remember, Geneva, this is a prestigious law school, not a professional basketball team."

Now, I wrote that as a fictional story, but that is what we get wherever we go. I used to say to my white colleagues at Harvard, "If I and the other black faculty at the time were crossing Massachusetts Avenue and got hit by a bus, you all couldn't get through the memorial service before you'd be looking for a replacement. Why do I have to get hit by a bus before they hire another black faculty member?"

When I look at black America today, I see a mixed picture. I see a great deal of progress by some, and I also see a condition that is perhaps not as bad as slavery, but fairly bad. Every time I help a girl of fifteen or sixteen years old up the subway stairs with her stroller—no man around, no ring on her finger—and she says, "Thank you, sir," my heart goes out, because I know she's not an individual case. The number of broken families, the increasing number of both black men and women in prisons, the young kids who get on the subway and only know about ten words, and three of them are *nigga*—these are the matters of great concern that leave me unable to appreciate fully the success of others, or even my own success. We've made it this far, yes, and I think we've got to keep on, but there certainly are casualties.

Chapter Thirteen

SUPPOSE

> TO BE SURE, BEHIND THE THOUGHT LURKS THE AFTER-
> THOUGHT—SUPPOSE, AFTER ALL, THE WORLD IS RIGHT
> AND WE ARE LESS THAN MEN? SUPPOSE THIS MAD IM-
> PULSE WITHIN US IS ALL WRONG, SOME MOCK MIRAGE
> FROM THE UNTRUE?
>
> —"Of the Training of Black Men"

In 1995, my birth mother, Tess, wrote a book about her choice to give me up for adoption, our reunion eleven years later, and our subsequent fifteen-year relationship. My willingness to participate in media publicity had been something of a deal breaker during the contract negotiations, and I had agreed, for the most part, without giving it a second thought. Despite fifteen years of painful dissonance and emotionally charged expectations between us, we had shared considerable joy and growth and laughter. Besides which, she was everything to me. And because I knew how strongly she felt about writing the book, I wanted to support her in that effort.

Even though I had not read the manuscript from cover to cover, I had allowed for a much-edited version of an afterword by me to appear as the book's final comment. After the book's publication, we launched a three-day publicity junket in New York City, which included a taping with NPR's "Terry Gross," an appearance on *Good Morning America*, and interviews with a handful of local and national newspapers. I believe it was one of the newspaper interviewers who asked me how I identified myself, given that I was of mixed race, had been raised by white adoptive parents, and, on the face of it, had later been reclaimed and reparented by a white birth mother. I told the reporter that I identified myself as a black woman, and by that point in my life, I did. Whether or not I felt like a black woman, or knew what it meant to be one, was perhaps a different matter altogether. But for certain, I identified myself as such.

That night over a celebration dinner at the swanky Upper East Side restaurant Elaine's, Tess told me that she had been uncomfortable with something I had said to one of the reporters earlier. "Oh?" I said, thinking she was probably going to chide me for hogging airtime, or for not deferring to her enough during the interview, or for mispronouncing or misarticulating an important meaning or message, or for being overly presumptuous about the reporter's interest in me.

"I would appreciate it," she said, "if you didn't go around calling yourself black."

"I'm sorry?"

"You came out of my body, and I am white."

It was a stunning moment for me, because it seemed—especially after years of increasingly heightened anxiety surrounding the issue of my racial identity—that I should be able to call myself whatever I wanted. And I had chosen to call myself black. Not biracial, not mixed, certainly not white, but straight-up black; it was easier, made sense to me, and felt right. Identifying myself as black was my prerogative. It also made me feel as though I was somehow able to disrupt the inevitable prejudice assigned to me, because even as I understood that I would forever be categorically perceived as black by contemporary culture and the Census Bureau, it mattered to me that I make the decision to be black on my own terms. It was a relief. I had not had the courage or the wherewithal to call myself black when I was growing up, but I knew all along that black was what I was. And now, suddenly, the woman who had given birth to me was telling me I was not black at all—that, in fact, it was a virtual impossibility.

In the essay "Of the Training of Black Men," Du Bois posits the following uncertainty: "Suppose this mad impulse within us is all wrong, some mock mirage from the untrue." He is talking about the impulse of black Americans to be treated as human beings. My mad impulse was different, though perhaps about as intuitive. Here I had taken twenty-five years to get comfortable with the idea of my blackness, and the one person who couldn't really be argued with as far as my origin was concerned was telling me that, comfortable or uncomfortable, the idea was just an idea. In effect, my sense of self was merely an illusion.

There is, then, an underlying objective in Du Bois's strange yet deeply compassionate musing, and that is addressed to black Americans: If at any time you rest easy that you are worthy as a human being, remember that there are unexpected and indomitable voices ready to remind you that you are not.

The myth of the Venus Hottentot, or the Hottentot Venus, and the social construction of the black female body in America as a vehicle of uncontrollable sexual desire, is born out of a real life, a real experience, and a real woman. She was known as Saartje Baartman, a Khoi woman born in Cape Town, South Africa, in the late 1700s, then taken to London in the early 1800s and exhibited as a freak show to satisfy Europe's then morbid fascination with the genitalia of South African women. Her exhibition did not prove successful, though, and she was sold off to an animal trainer in France. After her unexplained death in 1816, her genitals were cut off and presented to the Academy of Science as proof that Khoi women were not human.

It has been said that Saartje Baartman was enticed to London by the promise of fortune for merely allowing people to look at her body. Whether she was enticed or forced or taken, however she arrived in London, it is fairly certain that she did not anticipate being treated like an animal, or objectified as something she could not possibly have felt herself to be—nonhuman. There is no record of a first-person account from Baartman, no record of her own voice or perspective.

In 1990, the poet, playwright, and essayist Elizabeth Alexander introduced with the title poem of her groundbreaking collection of poetry, *The Venus Hottentot*, an idea of what that first-person account from Baartman might sound like: "I am called 'Venus Hottentot.'/I left Capetown with a promise of revenue. . . . I would return to my family a duchess, with watered-silk/dresses and money to grow food,/rouge and powders in glass pots. . . . That was years ago. . . . A professional animal trainer shouts my cues."

Like the black Americans in Du Bois's "Of the Training of Black Men," freed of chains and ready to put into practice a life of self-worth, Saartje Baartman indulged the same natural longing. And so, too, did I. It is the urge to be wholly of oneself, self-defined, and regarded as human.

Elizabeth Alexander

i came to the Venus Hottentot through scholarly reading and research, and so she was really just an idea to me at first, to echo that Du Boisian language of instinct and identity. I found everything I could about her that was available, which wasn't a whole lot at the time, the late eighties, and what seemed absent, of course, was her voice—her interior, her *self,* who she actually was, not just things about her and not just a self seen. This is what I've come to believe poetry can bring to history: We can imagine those voices that we might not have on the historical record. We don't have her diaries or letters, but in poetry, or in the theater or in fiction, for that matter, we can imagine in an informed way what that voice and perspective might have been. That was the challenge that I couldn't ignore. Then she began to speak to me, and the first line that she spoke was, "I am called the Venus Hottentot."

There's that great black vernacular expression, "Don't call me out of my name," and I thought, Here is someone for whom we don't have the name her mother and father gave to her. We know that she was called Venus Hottentot, we know that in Europe she was called Sara Baartman, we know that in Afrikaans she was called Saartje Baartman, but we don't have her Khoisan name, the name her parents wanted her to have. So that seemed an amazing starting place—to think about that kind of conundrum, and then to move on from there.

I didn't actually know what was driving me while I was writing the poem, but I did realize after the fact that there was something I understood very profoundly about being a young black woman who was sometimes seen as a racialized, sexualized spectacle, in a way that I think most young black women have experienced themselves at some point. It is that way in which the gaze racializes and sexualizes you when you don't want to be racialized or sexualized. But that wasn't something I was prepared to write about in the voice that was me, Elizabeth, in 1987.

And so, in terms of Du Bois, even as we may walk

around thinking of ourselves as racially complicated people, what does it mean in this postidentity era to stand the ground of our blackness nonetheless? What does it mean to say, "Maybe this is not all pathological, or not so essentialist that it obliterates the complexities of identity"? What does it mean to sit with and contemplate our complicated blackness? I think that is a very important ground to mark these days, because a lot of the current discourse on the subject can be dangerous. Certainly as it is played out in some academic circles, where we sometimes have gender studies and race studies that have very little to do with women and black people, there is this idea that we can somehow move beyond our identities instead of moving beyond the *limitations* of our identities. I don't think we ever can move beyond our identities. I think what we can do is simply continue to define ourselves in our multifacetedness.

Back, then, to Du Bois and the inherent question as to whether or not we deserve to be here. My own personal impulse has always been to go back and look at the flip side: How have we survived despite all of the incredibly concerted soul- and body- and identity-killing efforts that has been visited upon us? That's what I find most remarkable: Why are we still here? What does it really mean—and not in a glib, sloganistic sort of way—to be the children of survivors, to be the ones who survived, when you look at the odds not just of surviving the Middle Passage but of surviving slavery; not just surviving lynching and segregation but surviving the ongoing legacy of spirit killing?

If we are wrong about being here, so what if we are? Because the ongoing effort is, and will be, how we can continue to bolster our communities without being unduly nationalistic, because many nationalisms have a simple-mindedness to them that I don't necessarily think helps children to be critical thinkers and strong people. How do we teach our children to be aware, to question, to be tolerant, to be resilient and righteous? How do we nurture their brilliance and bravery?

For those of us whose day-to-day experiences are racialized, we nonetheless all have dream space, private space. I don't think that that space is raceless, or that it is without markers of identity, but I do think it's a space where those markers are rich, complicated, and not always resolved. That doesn't mean that there aren't ways in which we sometimes work collectively and let some of our complexities fall away because we want to get something done, but I do believe that the overall quest should be for everybody to feel that they have access to the private, complicated space within them.

My parents are race people. I come from race people. So there was always the sense that we had a responsibility, and some of that responsibility was simply to be civilized. We were aware, and I don't mean this in a cosmetic way, that we had to do well and to do a good job—to represent. That was always clear. I don't think it ever even had to be articulated. It was never articulated to me that we had to be twice as good as white people, but that was absolutely imparted nonetheless. There would be challenges, and so therefore we had to be prepared. We couldn't be raggedy in any way. And there was always a sense in both the way my parents were in the world and what they did for and with other people that you had a responsibility to share your privileges and gifts, whatever it was that you had, but particularly with other black people.

I grew up in Washington, D.C., during the 1960s and 1970s, and the idea was that we were firmly marching toward the sunlight. We were "overcoming." My parents were integrationists. They believed that we were changing history. When my father went to college, they wouldn't give him a white roommate. When I went to college, anybody could be your roommate. There was clear progress being made. It was the era of Martin Luther King, Jr.

People in my family had known Du Bois, so he was known to me as "Dr. Du Bois." One of my great-aunts would sometimes refer to him as "Dr. Dubious," because she didn't agree with some of his ideas. I don't know what those particular ideas were, but when you have someone who was as productive as he was, for as long a span of time as he was, and as certain of himself as he was, I think there were many people who might consider themselves as generally in his camp but who also had various ideological skirmishes with him. So that's how I first knew of Du Bois—that he was someone you didn't call W. E. B.

Du Bois, that you called him Dr. Du Bois, and that the "Dr." part was important. He was someone we were proud of, and critically engaged with.

One thing I remember that struck me about Du Bois and *The Souls of Black Folk* was his description of coming from Massachusetts and going to Fisk. That spoke to me, because as I began to study black literature as part of my undergraduate education, I was at the same time taking it very much into my own identity. The family joke was always, "We sent her off to Yale University and that's where she became *really* black." In this intensive study of black culture, I was taking all that I was reading and, first of all, finding what would be my life's work and great abiding love, but it was also helping me to think about what it meant to be a black person in unstereotypical terms.

I had gone to prep school in Washington and to other schools with mostly white kids, and reading Du Bois, I saw this great race man who had grown up in a white environment—and the miracle for him was going to Fisk and discovering this whole wide spectrum of black beauty. He was just blown away by it. The idea was amazing to me that someone could come into racial consciousness at that point in his life—in other words, that it wasn't something you were born with and had a clear sense of from the beginning, something that was always with you, and you knew what it meant to be your kind of black person—here Du Bois was in process. And now we think of him as the greatest race man of the twentieth century.

One of the things I think about today in terms of Du Bois is that he really set a very high standard for getting one's work done. There is a wonderful Du Bois statistic—I don't remember it precisely or where it comes from—that says when you average out everything that he ever wrote, that he published an article or an essay or a letter to the editor, or a story, or a book, something like once a week for his entire adult life. It's plausible, when you consider his body of work. That tells me that he was able to sit down at the typewriter and simply ask himself what he thought, and trust that his thinking and studying, and all that he knew, would be available to him when he was ready to write what he needed to write. There didn't seem to be a whole lot of agonizing for Du Bois about footnotes or whether or not people would agree or disagree with him. He just committed himself to the word, and put it out in the world. And so now we have an incredible record of a productive life's work, but more important, he weighed in on the issues of the day for something like seventy years—and I think that's very important, because so much of our good thinking and good energy as black people hasn't made its way to publication.

There are reasons that so much of our history has been expunged or wasn't recorded in the first place. The call of history is a chasm that's just waiting to be filled, for the dots to be connected. So to have that written record from Du Bois, that archive, for black people is especially precious. If you think about all the black lives that we don't have in biography form—you could write about incredible black people for the rest of your life in any particular area and never have enough time to do it. If you can accept that there is never enough time and never enough on record, then you can begin the hard, good work of adding to the record, and that will be enough.

Chapter Fourteen

HIGHER INDIVIDUALISM

ABOVE OUR MODERN SOCIALISM, AND OUT OF THE WOR-
SHIP OF THE MASS, MUST PERSIST AND EVOLVE THAT
HIGHER INDIVIDUALISM WHICH THE CENTERS OF CULTURE
PROTECT; THERE MUST BE A LOFTIER RESPECT FOR THE
SOVEREIGN SOUL THAT SEEKS TO KNOW ITSELF AND THE
WORLD ABOUT IT; THAT SEEKS A FREEDOM FOR EXPAN-
SION AND SELF-DEVELOPMENT; THAT WILL LOVE AND
HATE AND LABOR IN ITS OWN WAY, UNTRAMMELED ALIKE
BY OLD AND NEW.

—"Of the Training of Black Men"

At my ten-year high school reunion, an acquaintance made
mention of an article I'd recently written about growing up
black in New Hampshire. He said my perception was skewed if

I thought that he and anyone else at school had treated me differently because I was black. He said that, at least for his part, he had always treated me as a person and not as a black person, and he was hurt that I thought otherwise.

In the article he was talking about, I had written about my feelings of not being able to escape the color of my skin, while also not feeling comfortable living in it. But, perhaps this friend had a point. Maybe I had, in retrospect and unknowingly, turned my sense of insecurity as a regular high school teenager into an issue of race for no real reason. If no one saw me as black, then how could I be the victim of racial prejudice? I suddenly recalled a conversation from my senior year, when a friend had said to me, "Why is it always about race for you, Beck? I mean, give it a rest. It's not all about race."

Strangely, I don't remember it ever being all about race for me in high school. I remember pushing race aside until I couldn't push it anymore, or it wouldn't let me push. I remember feeling marked by my skin color no matter how gregariously I tried to press my individual personality. I remember wanting a boyfriend and not having one despite being told more than once by the all white boys I went to school with and had crushes on that I was one of the prettiest girls they had ever seen. I remember that a friend walked out of a class we had together because of a racist remark made by the teacher, long before it had even occurred to me to respond. Later, I was questioned by that same friend as to why I hadn't appeared more offended. I remember thinking then that if some of the things I was experiencing were not about race, then I must be an awful, unlovable, and unknowable person. But mostly, I remember thinking that I would be happy as heaven for it to not be all about race.

Not about race? Sign me up.

The truth is, it's a lot of work for things to be all about race, and I wasn't terribly interested in exerting too much effort when I was in high school. I wanted to be popular and to do well on tests and get invited to parties and be the kind of person that everyone thought was cool and fun to be around. I simply wanted people to see me. Neither, though, was it more admirable than that. It was not, as Du Bois exerted, the pursuit of a "higher individualism which the centers of culture protect." I would, however, consider my teenage desire to be seen and known as a way of seeking "a freedom for expansion and self-development . . . that will love and hate and labor in its own way, untrammeled alike by old and new."

Clarence Major, a true Renaissance man with gifted and celebrated talents as a painter, writer, and poet, could almost single-handedly represent the pursuit of higher individualism. His written work, for example, which includes several collections of poetry, a dictionary of African American slang, and experimental novels such as *All-Night Visitors* and *Painted Turtle*, clearly and with unfailing consistency presents an unusual voice, or voices, dynamic and ambitious, always with a great respect for the many and diverse leanings of the individual spirit.

Major resists the idea of being or producing anything inherently "black," although he acknowledges that there are those who do, many of whom exist as characters in his books. In a review for the *New York Times*, Richard Perry wrote of Major's earlier novel, *My Amputations*, that it was a book "in which the question of identity throbs like an infected tooth." One might naturally assume then that such a palpable description of identity struggle would translate back to the author who wrote it. But Major crafts characters so uniquely themselves, so fully formed, that the more sensible assumption would be to credit Major's genuine, multidimensional individuality as the foundation from which he creates the wholeness of others outside of himself.

Clarence Major

it's been a while since I've read *The Souls of Black Folk*, but my feeling is that it spoke largely to the education of black people, and also to the relationship between black people and academic life. In terms of a higher individualism, I think what Du Bois was really getting at comes toward the end of the essay "Of the Training of Black Men"—"black men must have respect: the rich and bitter depth of their experience, the unknown treasures of their inner life, the strange rendings of nature they have seen, may give the world new points of view and make their loving, living, and doing precious to all human hearts." What he was getting at, although he doesn't say it explicitly, is that there is a responsibility on the part of what he else-where calls the "Talented Tenth"—a responsibility toward those less fortunate members of the race.

The meaning of the "Talented Tenth" can certainly be broadened in contemporary terms, but during the time that Du Bois wrote about it, I don't think he was talking exclu-sively about elitism, even though in many ways, of course, he himself was something of an elitist. Du Bois had enough wisdom and objectivity to see beyond his own limitations as a person, far enough beyond to see the greater need for reaching past the difficulties of class. He hoped for a system of education that would generate not the kind of race con-sciousness that Booker T. Washington had in mind, whereby black Americans needed to be pulled up, but the kind of race consciousness that allowed for black Americans to evolve as individuals. It was a worthy go, but I don't think it has happened to any satisfactory degree—perhaps for some people, but not in terms of the masses, no.

It's a very complicated situation as to why black Americans at large have not been able to or have not cho-sen to pursue a path of higher individualism. Certainly racism plays a part, but there are other social issues at work—capitalism itself requires a large permanent under-class in order to function. And, unfortunately, black peo-ple have always been stuck in that underclass, and there have been all kinds of consistent forces at work to keep us there. In the arena of education, employment, and just about anywhere you turn, you are going to find forces working against efforts to change that disadvantage.

Du Bois, in his effort to change the conditions for black America, suggests the idea of modern socialism. American society may have always had a sort of socialist impulse within the capitalist construct, but it has never been able to fully realize that impulse. All you have to do is think about how difficult it is to get the government to approve medical care for everybody, a very simple matter, one that other countries have no problem with. It's just a simple issue: People should have a certain amount of medical care.

Of course there are things about capitalism that have served me, yes, certainly, but I suppose ideally what I would like is some sort of happy wedding between socialism and capitalism. I don't want to put words in his mouth, but I think *that* is the idea Du Bois was leaning toward all of his life, and by the time he moved to Africa, he was definitely all the way there. The core issue in *Souls*, and particularly in the passage about higher individualism, is about creating a kind of social and domestic environment in which the black individual can find nourishment—intellectually, artistically, emotionally, and aesthetically.

I have been lucky to make the kind of work I want to make, yes, but at what price? Whatever success I have, it wasn't supposed to happen. Somehow, I was able to slip through. Of course I persevered, and talent is part of it, but a lot of people have talent. It wasn't easy to create an environment for myself in which I could feel nourished. I grew up on the South Side of Chicago in the 1940s and 1950s, where the value system is no different from that which all America most cherishes—a value system driven by materialism and profit. You can't succeed, certainly not as an artist, or a writer, or a poet, with those kinds of values. You can't write with money in mind. You can't paint with money in mind. You can't create poetry with money as an objective. You can hope that there will be some kind of financial reward, but it can't be central to your life if you want to be a creative person.

I survive pretty well now, and I have for a number of years, but in the beginning it was pretty much a hand-to-mouth existence. Fortunately, I came along at a time when universities were beginning to take writers under their wings, and I got into the system fairly early. I know that a lot of people felt then and feel now that the university is no place for an artist, no place for a poet, no place for a writer. But I disagree. It's perhaps the only thing we have to offer in this country that provides a kind of safe haven for creative people. In the days of the Harlem Renaissance, there were other ways of being financed—patrons, for example. Now we do what we can do to get our work done.

Do I think there is a particular way of producing culturally black art? It's interesting, because I was interviewing Jacob Lawrence some years ago, an interview that appeared in *The Black Scholar,* and I asked him the same question: "Is your art black art?" And he said no. I told him that I was surprised by his answer, and he said, "In America, anybody outside the culture can paint black figures. But because an African American is painting black figures, does that make it black art?" So, the only thing left is the stylistic, aesthetic issue. Lawrence did not feel that there were specific lines and colors that delineated African American art from American art. And I don't either, no.

In terms of books and writing, I think that there is a kind of tradition that goes back through to the nineteenth century, looking at people like Paul Lawrence Dunbar and Charles Chesnutt, and then later Nella Larsen and Zora Neale Hurston. Let me say this: You can identify ways of perception, ways of interpreting experience that could be considered uniquely African American. That said, I think it's hard to separate out European influences. In America, anybody who sets out to make something, be it art or literature, will inevitably end up creating something that represents the cross-fertilization that occurred at the beginning of this country's civilization. There's no way to avoid it.

Ralph Ellison, for example, who many people feel was too hung up on European writers, wasn't the only African American writer of his generation to look toward European writers as literary ancestors. This was true even of Richard Wright, who very often gets celebrated by Black Nationalists and descendants of Black Nationalists.

Upon close scrutiny, you will find that his roots come from very diverse places and not just the African American experience. James Baldwin, too, comes more specifically from Henry James than any other literary figure, black or white.

Emphasizing that which is uniquely black and that which isn't through art or books or magazines or churches, or whatever it may be, both nurtures black people and promotes a kind of separatism. Culture is an essential thing. One needs culture as a means of identifying who one is, where one is coming from, and who one aspires to be. At the same time, exclusive cultural identification is inherently limited. One of the beautiful things about evolving in the world is the possibility, the future, of an individual existence.

As Langston Hughes said about us, black people, in "The Negro Artist and the Racial Mountain," we are both beautiful and ugly, too. He meant it metaphorically, of course, but I have tried to remember that throughout my life, because as an artist or a writer, you can't afford to forget the humanity implied in that statement. You have to keep a clear vision of the full human being. That's what Hughes meant, and that's what Du Bois meant.

Chapter Fifteen

THE MOST BEAUTIFUL EXPRESSION

> AND SO BY FATEFUL CHANCE THE NEGRO FOLK-SONG—
> THE RHYTHMIC CRY OF THE SLAVE—STANDS TODAY NOT
> SIMPLY AS THE SOLE AMERICAN MUSIC, BUT AS THE MOST
> BEAUTIFUL EXPRESSION OF HUMAN EXPERIENCE BORN THIS
> SIDE OF THE SEAS.
>
> —"Of the Sorrow Songs"

It may sound foolish, but I can always find in music what it means to me to be black, whereas I can almost never find it in words. Maybe because music invites me to crawl inside, while words can't wait for me to stumble. At the end of the day, all the intellectualizing, posturing, and genuine hope for deliverance is nothing in the face of what happens to me when I hear

Nina Simone or Stevie Wonder, Wynton Marsalis, Bill Withers, A Tribe Called Quest, Roberta Flack, Al Green, De La Soul, Coltrane, or anything by Prince. I do also listen to, and love, music made by white people. I grew up in New Hampshire listening to the likes of Jackson Browne, Elton John, Linda Ronstadt, Fleetwood Mac, and the Eagles. I knew all the words to REO Speedwagon's "Take it on the Run" before my tenth birthday. But the moment I heard Stevie Wonder for the first time at my friend Shelby's house when we were both eleven years old, I understood immediately that this music resonated for me in a different way, the whole of it—the voice, the meter, the lilt, the struggle, the history, the blood, the swell, the soul, the beauty.

Black music is the only thing I don't mind people assuming I must enjoy like, say, watermelon, collard greens, and basketball. Maybe that's precisely why I like black music. Why should I care? To think that there are classes and majors and schools with the sole purpose of teaching the history and importance of where this music comes from makes me feel bad for the people who come into the world not already knowing.

Du Bois knew. "And so," he wrote in "Of the Sorrow Songs," the last essay in *Souls*, "by fateful chance the Negro folk-song—the rhythmic cry of the slave—stands today not simply as the sole American music, but as the most beautiful expression of human experience born this side of the seas." Du Bois was referring specifically to the slave spirituals or the "Sorrow Songs," as he called them, although contemporary black music today, whether it be hip-hop, jazz, R&B, or Lenny

Kravitz, amounts to the same thing—the same rhythmic cry, the same beautiful expression of human experience.

Whether you love or hate films made by Spike Lee, you cannot ignore the eerie, pitch-perfect scores that generally accompany them. Terence Blanchard is equally gifted as a film composer as he is a horn player, and he brings to both a kind of heart that is big with the pleasure of place and time. With reflective deference to the greats and a willingness to set a modern tone, Blanchard creates film scores that are full of sorrow as well as joy. Blanchard's Golden Globe–nominated score to Lee's *25th Hour* in 2002, which features daunting yet appropriate images of post-9/11 New York, and follows the final dreadful hours of a man sentenced to prison, could have told the story itself.

Terence Blanchard

When i moved to New York and got the chance to meet
and hang out with some of these guys I'd admired throughout my life, my first reaction was not "Who are these figures in a historical context?" It was, rather, "Damn, these
are the cats." I feel a connection to the history of our music through information passed on to me by my peers and
those who came before me. I've had stories handed down
to me through Art Blakey from Thelonius Monk, Louis
Armstrong, Charlie Parker; the list is endless. And I find
myself passing on the same stories, so it's like the old
African tradition of being a griot.

There's always been this mystical idea of what art is all about—that it's these deep flurries of unconscious thought being realized in some form of visual or musical expression. And that's true in some instances, but a lot of the time artists and jazz musicians are just regular people, and I think that's what makes the art and music more significant. Some artists may cultivate a solitary existence in their mind, but the things that really inspire what we do and that really motivate us are the same types of things that inspire and motivate everybody—food, family, history, culture, seeing beautiful places. Without that, I don't think people would relate to what we do.

Music is special for black people because that's where our culture in America started. We weren't allowed to write; the only thing we were allowed to do was sing. And so through that came all the pain and joy of everything that we experienced. That cultural preservation in music is now part of black tradition, maybe even more so than it was back then. Music is the universal language no matter where you are from or what your history is, but the difference is in the intent, and in our culture the intent has always been to convey our experiences and emotions. I don't care whether you're listening to jazz, gospel, R&B, soul, funk, doesn't matter—that's the common denominator. That's what I hear.

I think it's unfair to place the burden on the musician to represent our culture at large, because musicians need to do what they're going to do. Now, if they're doing it to make money, then they've made their choice in life. That's not why I personally am in the music business, but I can't fault people who are. In terms of this era of music making, specifically hip-hop, I would hope that at least the initial intent is to enlighten. I listen to some of the cuts, and some of them have something important to say. The problem is that I don't think that those are the ones that get played.

Art Blakey used to tell me all the time, "Look, if you've got something to offer, then the world will lead a path to your door. But if you ain't got nothin' to offer, then you got some work to do." When Wynton, Branford, all of us, when we were in New Orleans starting out, we never thought of ourselves as becoming this successful. We wanted to play music; we wanted to play jazz. We always thought we'd end up playing studio music to make enough money so that we could keep playing live gigs on the weekends. That's where our heads were. So when the success started to come, it was just as much of a shock to me as it was to anybody else. Then you start to roll with it because you get these great and interesting opportunities, like playing with Sonny Rollins at Carnegie Hall, meeting and playing with Dizzy Gillespie, or hanging with Miles Davis.

Most people recognize the fact that I've scored all these films, more so than the jazz I've put out on regular albums, and that's fine. To me, scoring a film is like being in a good band. If you're in a good band and you play a tune, you don't take the first solo. Somebody else takes the first solo. If that person plays a great solo, then that inspires you to do the same. It's not a competitive thing; it's a collaborative thing. It makes you rise to a higher level. That's the kind of experience I've had when I worked with Spike on his films, where I know that I have to do a lot of homework, and know what I'm talking about. When you look at Spike's films, you've got actors who are doing great work, you've got a beautifully shot film—from Ernest Dickerson all the way up to this cinematographer he's using now, Rodrigo Prieto—there's great editing, all the scenes have an interesting look to them, and, of course, the direction is great. And then Spike hands it to me. You don't want to drop the ball.

You tell a story when you compose a film score, but you also tell a story when you play a concert set. The difference is that the film score is someone else's story and the concert set is mine. It's an old cliché, but the story of playing in a band is the story of how I'm feeling that day. I've just been in the recording studio for the past week or so, and one of the things that is frustrating about recording is that we're not necessarily capturing what we do live. Musically it's still good, but it's just one facet of the band. When we play live, we stretch things out, we play longer, and we experiment. When we record, you have to tighten all that up and bring things into focus. So rather than an extended narrative, like when we're playing live, the music we record in the studio is more like a poem.

Wayne Shorter told me something that really stuck

with me; it was a story about a woman who had suffered a lot of problems in her artistic career and had almost reached the point of suicide, and her mother said to her, "Baby, you got to have courage to be happy." That statement just stayed with me, and I realized that you need courage not only to be happy but to be human, and to be who you are. Initially, I hope people get more of a feeling than a meaning from my music, because that's what draws people back. And through being drawn to something, then you can hope to find some meaning. It's like when you fall in love: You are first attracted to a physical beauty or something in that person's personality, but it isn't until much later that the relationship can develop and demonstrate its meaning to you.

There are a lot of people who will never seek out the truth about a person or a type of music or a movement for themselves. They will forever accept what other people tell them, without ever questioning it. Jazz musicians go to a lot of places that most black musicians would never go, like Platteville, Wisconsin, you dig? I was just there for three days. And when you look at audiences in a place like that, you see how difficult it is going to be to change the perception about jazz. But, in general, I see a lot more young African American people coming to my gigs.

The thing that's interesting about being an instrumentalist is that the messages are very abstract. While most people relate to vocal music, because it's something they can immediately grasp, and while I love the voice and feel it is perhaps the most expressive instrument on the planet, words are still limiting. There are certain things that we feel that can't be described through words—something in between love and hate, sorrow and joy. Even if we find the words that we think might describe what we're feeling, that still isn't it. And in that space that we can't describe in words, there is room for magic.

Chapter Sixteen

THE PREACHER MAN

> THE PREACHER IS THE MOST UNIQUE PERSONALITY DE-
> VELOPED BY THE NEGRO ON AMERICAN SOIL. A LEADER, A
> POLITICIAN, AN ORATOR, A "BOSS," AN INTRIGUER, AN IDE-
> ALIST—ALL THESE HE IS, AND EVER, TOO, THE CENTER OF
> A GROUP OF MEN, NOW TWENTY, NOW A THOUSAND IN
> NUMBER.
>
> —"Of the Faith of the Fathers"

I don't know religion from Adam. My parents both left the Catholic church shortly after they were married, and my birth mother, Tess, was always more inclined toward nobility than religion. By the time I was thirty, I had been to exactly one church service, some sort of Easter service at the Episcopal church of a friend in middle school, although, well into my

adult life, I had heard stories from friends and peers and colleagues about the black church experience. Certainly, I understood the significance of religion in African American history,
and it made sense to me that religion, faith, and so on would
play a strong role for black people who suffered through slavery. But I preferred to credit their survival more to individual
will and tenacity than to guidance from God.

Aside from a general lack of interest in religion, the black
church—black churchgoing folk and prominent black figures in
the church community—seemed a business not to mess with,
a matter inappropriate for experimentation. So I kept my distance from it until a boyfriend of mine, a white boyfriend, suggested we go to see the Brooklyn Tabernacle Choir one
Sunday morning.

"You've seen them, haven't you?" I told him that I hadn't.
"Well, you've heard of them, right?" It rang vaguely familiar,
yes, I said. He insisted we go.

The Brooklyn Tabernacle Choir performs at the Brooklyn
Tabernacle Church on Flatbush Avenue in Brooklyn, New York,
not very far from where I was living at the time. When you go,
it seems that in general you have to stand in line or take a
number or watch a closed-circuit broadcast from the street. In
any case, they don't perform right away. First, a sermon is
given. I don't remember the name of the preacher giving the
sermon on that day, but he rose to the microphone and asked
us with clear and vigorous intent to "Praise Jesus!" Bodies rose
up around me, and in less than a minute, the whole congregation was standing, echoing the preacher's words, waving

gloved hands, nodding hat-adorned heads, eyes closed—a faith supreme. I looked over and saw that my boyfriend was standing, too, all six white gangly feet of him, swaying smoothly within the heat and murmur and energy of the crowd.

I stood reluctantly, hands in my pockets, self-conscious, trying to be cool. I stood like that for maybe fifteen minutes before I realized that nobody was trying to look at me. It was not about what I was doing or how I was responding or what I looked like if and when I was striving to feel God's presence. It was about faith and trust and celebration, led by a man whose voice provided a well-lighted tunnel through which people could travel to where they needed to go. He was, of course, preaching God's word, but he also appeared to be holding the hand of everyone in that congregation, holding it tightly, and showing people a way. Not *the* way, but *a* way.

Du Bois's sense of the Negro preacher as "the most unique personality developed by the Negro on American Soil. A leader, a politician, an orator, a 'boss,' an intriguer, an idealist" is perhaps among the more accessible of his prophetic observations that still hold up today. There are few people in America who don't like, or who aren't at least in some way drawn to, a black preacher. The characteristic style of a historically traditional black preacher, which downright lifts, tells, and chants—does everything short of physically giving God's word—evokes a trust that goes beyond common faith and worship. The black preacher's confidence is palpable, his mission unwavering.

The Reverend James Forbes, who is the Senior Minister of

Riverside Church in New York, gives sermons that transport you back to a time you can't remember being in but where you know you've been. His sermons rich with allegoric references and gentle, humanistic values, the Reverend Forbes embodies the spirit of the legendary black preacher while also engendering a kind of innovative spiritualism not just for black people but for an entire populace.

The Reverend James Forbes

To my mind, the black preacher is born out of the African figure known as the griot, a figure who served in African communities as the expression of the continuity of things eternal. In contemporary terms, I don't think very many people understand that historic influence, and so they are not aware that whatever a black preacher is doing at any given time cannot be extracted or excerpted from the consciousness of the community he is serving. It's like when you see someone give someone else a kiss— you focus on that gesture, but you know nothing about the history of their relationship or their struggles. Anyone who looks at preaching primarily as a moment of verbal exchange misses out on what is really going on. It is also among the surest kind of evidence that black Americans are ahistoric.

We became ahistorical when we were taken from the shores of Africa and learned how to escape the brutality of slave consciousness by allowing for the erasure of our past. Although there are conversations about Africanism today, back then we did not cultivate the consciousness of our relationship to Africa. Rather, we tried to place roots in the unwelcoming terrain of America, so fixed on what might be beyond this veil of tears that the roots were not sunk deep enough to take hold even had the terrain been welcoming. We wanted to survive. We didn't want to think about what came before, what we had left behind and were forced to endure—an experience that has since been influenced by the suggestion that we were being done a favor by being brought over here. So you see that any lingering sense of our past has been contaminated.

Without a continuous historic consciousness, preaching, like our culture, also becomes ahistorical, and participates in the escapism so frequently experienced in the black church. Somewhere along the way, the art of preaching became the facilitation of denial, if only for the thirty minutes the preacher preaches. Let's say that after you have an operation, the doctors let you punch the medication, but only while you're in the hospital, because they know they can detoxify you fast enough if need be. But if when you go home, you ask for your own bag of morphine to take with you, they've got a junkie on their hands. A deadening of the senses so that the pain is endurable is fine, but when that begins to reprint itself on a form such as preaching, which was originally as expansive as time and eternity itself, anytime you administer palliatives, you are cheapening the experience.

The black church in America started out as an alternative island of consciousness for pain. And when anyone is in a situation of agonizing pain, it's not for those of us who have some relative comfort to deny them that which at least sustains them. But the horror is to have a regimen for sustaining a state of being in pain when you are called upon to move toward wholeness. So, then, the black preacher has to make a decision: Does he want to equip people for the real world, or does he want to help them endure to the point of escape to a world that is yet to be?

Many years ago, Ossie Davis wrote a play called *Purlie Victorious*, and in it, the main character, Purlie, says, "Ain't no promise, no pie in the sky, no life ever after right after we die. I have a different banner to wave . . . you and me we do the best we can . . . make way for a new fangled preacher man." The challenge was to say that this preacher stands in contrast to those who emerged to provide escapism during the nightmarish horror of slavery. This is not to say that those earlier preachers did not serve a purpose—had they not existed, maybe we would not have come forth to imagine that there is a new way that preaching might serve the community.

I cannot afford to underestimate the power of stress reduction that is administered by the church. We now know that whatever we are struggling through, stress exacerbates it. So I say that if the only thing I do is to render a season of stress-reduced euphoria, then that is enough. That is as valuable as aspirin. And that is why we need to celebrate the black church, and to see it as lifesaving, while still being able to ask whether it is possible to become habituated to methods that were designed to sustain us only until we believed we could walk again. The black church provides a place where we can sit outside of the negation of who we have become, and it forces us to create an alternative against what is offered by the majority culture. It is the recognition that what is good news for the oppressor cannot be good news for the oppressed. It is the recognition that there had to be a homegrown variety of biblical interpretations.

The image of the black preacher that is strongest for me is one that comes from a Gullah folktale that appears in the 1950s Negro folklore collection by Langston Hughes and Arna Bontemps. It starts like this: "Once all Africans could fly like birds." In the story, a slave woman has just given birth and is beaten down and beaten down by the overseer, when an old black man says the words "Kum Buba Yali," which means "Let them go up on high," and she, with the baby at her side, flies off into the sky. When the overseer discovers what is going on, he says, "Get that black devil, he's the one who's causing us to lose all our slaves!" The old man turns to the rest of the black people in the field and says something that the overseer does not understand, because he is speaking to his people in the language of their mothers and fathers, and they all fly away.

That is what the preacher does. He speaks the language of our mothers and fathers, in the field, in solidarity with the slaves, in anticipation of being asked whether it is time for strategic planning in regard to the eventual revoke that a spirit has in mind. Preaching is a message of liberation or it is a message of sustenance. But it is damnable to be primarily a preacher of patient endurance when the prospect of liberation is present. To be a preacher is to be given a gift.

Afrocentric religion does not have the tradition between sacred and secular, and therefore, all of life is sacred. During summers in West Africa, where I spent some time as a young man, the village would have a yam festival to celebrate harvesting the yams. This was a religious expression. They did not have to go to church. You went to the yam festival and you heard the griot tell the story of how he dare not take the first harvest of the yam without remembering that the harvest is not automatic, that it is because of the ancestors, those who came before. The griot tells of the many times of droughts and famine throughout the years, but that because people have lived in conformity with the principles of the elders, this year we have been blessed. The griot is the lead teller of the story, but the rest of the people are singing, praising, and nodding along as he's telling it, so that it is not his story alone, but the community's story as a whole.

And so African religious expression has always been participatory. Some black people think that the worst thing Du Bois wrote in *Souls* was about the "frenzy of a Negro revival"—the dancing, the shouting, and the catching up into ecstasy. They think if white people or Europeans read that, they would get the sense that we are victims of uncontrolled excess. I think that when I get touched by the spirit, my traditional rules and motor actions are transcended and a new freedom comes.

As a culture, I think black people are lost. We have been granted the illusion of power and incorporation into the benefits of power, and we have bought into that illusion. Rather than Du Bois's "double-consciousness," we now have what I call cognitive dissidence. Somewhere inside, we know that the trophies offered to us are hollow, and yet we go for them anyway, because of the power of manna. And this brings us right back to where we started—erasing our history, and trying to plant roots into infertile terrain.

The black church today will tell you that, yes, you need to survive, but you also need to preserve the riches of your heritage. Riverside Church in New York, where I preach, is an integrated church, which can introduce problems—white people do not need someone to say "Kum Buba Yali." But I am convinced that we need not be reductionist about spiritual growth, because we're all bound now.

Chapter Seventeen

WHAT SOUL I WILL

I SIT WITH SHAKESPEARE AND HE WINCES NOT. ACROSS
THE COLOR LINE I MOVE ARM IN ARM WITH BALZAC AND
DUMAS. . . . FROM OUT OF THE CAVES OF EVENING THAT
SWING BETWEEN THE STRONG-LIMBED EARTH AND THE
TRACERY OF THE STARS, I SUMMON ARISTOTLE AND
AURELIUS AND WHAT SOUL I WILL, AND THEY COME ALL
GRACIOUSLY WITH NO SCORN OR CONDESCENSION.

—"Of the Training of Black Men"

I had never acted on-screen until I was given a role in Sherman
Alexie's 2002 independent film, *The Business of Fancydancing*.
But, when I got the script in 2001, I could relate to and understand every single word written. It is a beautifully told story
about cultural identity, anger, and resentment, and I was sure

that I would be able to deliver a performance true to the character as conceived by the writer/director. My character was the judge and the judgement at the center of the narrative—she was all-knowing, arrogant, dynamic, and could arbitrarily inflict irreparable emotional damage on anyone within close-enough proximity. My sense when I first read the script was that the race of this character wasn't as important as the power of her wrath. Full disclosure: The writer/director Sherman Alexie is a friend, and he wrote the part for me. Even though it would be obvious to most that if he'd written the role for me, then he'd written the role for a black woman, this had not especially registered with me until we started shooting.

My first scene was the hardest and longest of the twelve that featured my character. It was a monologue, an oration, a performance within a performance. The set was spare, with a black backdrop, a spotlight, and a vintage-style microphone stand. My character was meant to step into the spotlight and introduce an Indian violin virtuoso named Mouse, a slick, handsome, troubled, and sardonic young man who knew both his appeal and how to use it. The first take was okay, but the sound wasn't right, or we needed to try another angle. Whatever it was, I felt that I was very near the mark with my delivery. My voice, calm and resonant, announced the presence of Mouse in a way that made him my character's peer—someone she respected and would allow a seat at her table. But that was the wrong way to go, Sherman said. My character, he explained in so many words, sat at her table alone.

Even though I had completely memorized my lines, by the

fifth take I was reading from cue cards. We shot the scene maybe eight times before Sherman came over to me and whispered in my ear, "More righteous, more forceful—pretend you're Patricia Smith." As soon as he said that, I knew I was sunk and that this scene would never make it into the film. I couldn't pretend I was Patricia Smith. The very fact that he had to tell me to pretend I was Patricia Smith proved that I didn't have what it took to pretend I was Patricia Smith.

Patricia Smith is a woman who can take over a room inside of ten seconds, a woman who makes words think twice about coming out of anybody else's mouth, a woman with an unearthly understanding of language, and a woman who is, without question, a black woman. I felt I knew this about her without ever having met her.

Read any poem by Patricia Smith, or any article from 1994, when she was fired from the *Boston Globe* for embellishing stories for her "Metro" column, and you might experience a similar reaction to both—a sort of visceral yet tainted empathy, a dangerous and electrifying reverence, and the sense of being in the presence of a captured spirit with large, tethered, and bleeding wings. She has made mistakes. Big ones. Though even as I and many others have imposed upon her an idea of blackness, or as she may be perceived in a more recent social context as the pre–Jayson Blair scapegoat of the black journalism community, in the end, Patricia Smith wants what most black writers and artists and human beings, including Du Bois, dare to want, and that is a seat at the Big Table.

Du Bois translates this longing into metaphor, as envisioned in a dreamlike passage from "Of the Training of Black Men," pierced by deep sorrow and bold conviction: "I sit with Shakespeare and he winces not. Across the color line I move arm in arm with Balzac and Dumas. . . . From out the caves of evening that swing between the strong-limbed earth and the tracery of the stars, I summon Aristotle and Aurelius and what soul I will, and they come all graciously with no scorn or condescension."

Equality, shared billing, to be taken seriously. In the years since what is widely considered in the journalism community as her permanent fall from grace, Smith has been forthright about taking responsibility for her actions. She has also, though, remarked in a way that does not seem an attempt to justify her behavior that her ache for equality and her ambition to secure a seat at the Big Table were perhaps the main precipitating factors that contributed to her ultimate breach in judgment.

Patricia Smith

I'm just beginning to realize that people talk about me in terms of being this sort of fierce black woman poet. And it's funny to me that people think of my work as being particularly black. Before, and apart from, *Close to Death*, which is dedicated to my son and is meant to be a book of persona poems in the voices of black men, I certainly saw my poems stamped heavily with my signature—since I'm black, that's going to be there—but there are a lot of the poems that, unless you knew me, would not necessarily read as thought they were written by someone who is black. I actually flailed about with that realization for a while.

I grew up in a small family, and even though my mother was a native of Alabama, she was also ashamed of the South in many ways. Whenever I would start to ask her questions about my family tree, she would say, "Oh, you don't need to know about all that nonsense." So she sort of shut that portion of my history off. My mother was also the "always be respectful of white people" type of person. She would become very silent and kind of in awe when there were white people around. She used to call me at work and say, "Don't mess up that job those white people gave you." Whenever a white person paid more than cursory attention to you, whatever you could do to keep their attention, you did. So I grew up thinking that I needed to do whatever I needed to do to be accepted.

From the time that I was ten years old, my father stopped living with us. I think if my family would have stayed together, I might have been more of a well-rounded person in terms of my racial self, because my father, who was sort of a rogue, would sneak in from time to time and tell me I could do and be whatever I wanted. Luckily, although my parents were not able to live together, my father would visit every day. My mother was the disciplinarian—she would comb my hair, check my grades, take me to church, spank me—and my father was the frustrated blues singer. I have no idea how they ended up together.

We lived on the West Side of Chicago, and my parents knew that the key to success for me started with my getting out of there and going to a white school, any white school. I wound up going to one of the worst white schools in the city of Chicago, but there sure were a lot of white people. In my graduating class, there were eight hundred whites and twelve blacks. Every day I would ride across town, and I would always feel like I was one person when I got on the bus and somebody else when I got off.

The first thing I can remember writing was the ongoing story of my alter ego. Her name was Erica Donovan. Erica had very dark hair and very light blue eyes, which I thought was the most appealing combination. She had six incredibly handsome brothers. She was class valedictorian, head cheerleader, class *vice* president—I didn't want to get carried away. Her mother was a doctor and her father was a lawyer. All the colleges on earth wanted her to come to their school. And I would fill these notebooks with her adventures—Erica at cheerleader tryouts, and Erica deciding which of the twenty guys who asked her to the prom she's going to go with. I thought I was just writing about Erica until I realized how much I wanted to be her. I mean, I might have been able to identify with her, Erica and I may have wanted the same things, but I knew that my way of getting those things and Erica's way were going to be real different.

This is going to sound funny, but actually I don't know how I got smart and grew to love language. I can go back to teachers in grade school who encouraged me, but as far as loving language as much as I do, and having it hit me so hard, I don't know where that came from. It didn't come from my parents—my father was something of a story-teller, but my mother was not happening in that department. It's a mystery to me. And I have felt it from the beginning.

After I started writing poetry as an adult was when I read *The Souls of Black Folk* for the first time. It was recommended to me by a guy I met in Chicago once I discovered the poetry scene there. His name was Michael War, and for some strange reason he used to quote from *The Souls of Black Folk,* and finally I got so tired of pretending I knew what he was talking about that I finally just said to him, "Should I read this?" And he said, "Yes, we should all read it." I remember it later inspiring a couple of poems, because I think the first time you read *Souls*, you're like, "Of course!" Then you get angry at yourself because you think to yourself, I should have been putting this into words in different ways every day of my writing life, and I have not been doing that.

When I started writing poetry, in every poem I was really trying to say, "I own this world"—everything I look at, I can comment on, and that comment matters. And *Souls* was definitely fuel for me in that regard, because I felt like when I was in a roomful of people listening to me read my poetry that it was up to me to try to show them how to own the world, too. When I'm reading, I'm thinking about rubbing away the barriers. Du Bois does that in *Souls*.

If you call yourself a writer, and you say you're impassioned about writing, you should write in any way that is available to you. Poetry and journalism sort of came up parallel for me, but poetry, in retrospect, has always felt like home. There's no excuse for my actions at the *Boston Globe*, but the poetic element was exactly what people always said they liked best about my columns. I could have delivered that element without embellishing, and each time I tweaked a story, I thought it would be the last. That incident was about taking a stupid risk, and getting caught.

At the worst of it, I was crawling around the floor of my house. People were looking in my windows. *60 Minutes* was calling. It was crazy. My husband at the time said to me, "You've hurt and disappointed all your friends." Oprah's show called and said, "Oprah is doing a show on lying and wants to know if you'd like to be a guest." Oh yes, of course, please, can I? I mean, I had reached a point where I'd decided I just wasn't going to write anymore.

Then I started getting phone calls from poets, and I also got a card from the organizers of the National Poetry Slam, who encouraged me to participate, and that's when I realized that from the moment I discovered poets, I was closer to them than to my own family. The poetry community embraced me throughout the whole thing with the *Globe*, whereas people in the journalism community said things like "Well, what are you going to do now that you can't write anymore?" So I went to the Slam, and it was weird. I ended up crying, but it was healing, too. My experience at the *Globe* is in a safe place for me now; I'm okay. But it will never go away.

I've always been very aware of being how ever many people I need to be to get to the end of the day. I have made a lot of shifts in who I am, and even though it can start to feel that there is something wrong with that shifted self, the shifts I have made are important. A lot of people ask me who my favorite writers are, and for a long time I used to say Toni Morrison and Gwendolyn Brooks, but Toni Morrison and Gwendolyn Brooks are actually not my favorite writers. It was my automatic, "This is what I need to say because I'm black" response. I said it for years, so much so that I began to believe it.

Now, I really admire Toni Morrison, and I love Gwendolyn Brooks, but my two favorite writers are Stephen Dobbins, a white male poet, and James Lee Burke, a white male novelist. I identify strongly with the passion I see driving their words. I think that they would write in a dark, locked room—if they knew they would never get out, they would still write. Do I therefore say that because these two writers don't share the same racial or cultural background as I do, then that passion can't be real? No, I don't believe that. I'm forty-seven years old, and I've just now reached the point where I can say, Yes, my two favorite writers are white men.

Chapter Eighteen

THE HEALING

> IF, WHILE THE HEALING OF THIS VAST SORE IS PROGRESS-
> ING, THE RACES ARE TO LIVE FOR MANY YEARS SIDE BY
> SIDE, UNITED IN ECONOMIC EFFORT, OBEYING COMMON
> GOVERNMENT, SENSITIVE TO MUTUAL THOUGHT AND
> FEELING, YET SUBTLY AND SILENTLY SEPARATE IN MANY
> MATTERS OF DEEPER HUMAN INTIMACY,—IF THIS UN-
> USUAL AND DANGEROUS DEVELOPMENT IS TO PROGRESS
> AMID PEACE AND ORDER, MUTUAL RESPECT AND GROW-
> ING INTELLIGENCE, IT WILL CALL FOR SOCIAL SURGERY AT
> ONCE THE DELICATEST AND NICEST IN MODERN HISTORY.
> —"Of the Training of Black Men"

In the spring of 2003, I was invited to give a reading at the
Saratoga Springs Public Library in Saratoga Springs, New York.
Then in the early throes of shaping and writing this book, I

read from the prologue, which seemed the most cohesive bit of it at the time. Afterward, during the question-and-answer period, a white man who was probably in his mid to late sixties asked this question of me: "Clearly, you're intelligent and well educated, and have been given many opportunities in life—why don't you just call yourself white?"

The question did not stir any audible reaction from the rest of the audience, all mostly older and white, nor did it shock me. The man was sincere, and I think he really did wonder why I didn't call or consider myself white, given what I had articulated by way of the book's introductory remarks about my life experience and background. I treated the question like any other. "Because," I replied, "I live in contemporary American culture."

No matter how much time, how many words, how lengthy the analysis set to the issue of race and racial identity, there will still be the person who asks, as if it were the easiest thing in the world to parlay, why it can't just be this way or that way. The reasons why are many, but the reason that resonates most is as simple as it is complex.

Understanding race in America is, to use Du Bois's words, an "unusual and dangerous development." It is a work in progress, he continued, that "will call for social surgery at once the delicatest and nicest in modern history." Such a high-risk surgery requires the best surgeons and the most willing of patients. Even more risky is performing surgery on an already-open wound; a wound that refuses to heal.

LeAlan Jones, who first earned recognition as the thirteen-year-old coauthor of the book *Our America: Life on the*

Southside of Chicago (1997), represents a new generation of African American youth. His is a generation that embraces both Eminem and 50 Cent, *The Source* and *GQ*, *Survivor* and *The Bernie Mac Show*, and which is the target audience for newly multiculturalized megamovie franchises such as *The Matrix* and *Charlie's Angels*.

After we finished our interview on a bench in New York's Union Square last year, LeAlan and I lingered for a while. Friendly but not close, we hadn't seen each other in quite a while and so were just catching up, very casually, when mid-sentence, almost as if it were part of what he was saying to me, LeAlan looked up past my shoulder and said, "Hey, Q-Tizzy, what up?" Then, in this one beautiful seamless motion, LeAlan and the man he had just greeted exchanged the graceful palm-to-fingers slide of a familiar handshake, the man kept on walking, and LeAlan resumed the sentence where he'd left off with me. A little while later, having recognized the man he'd shaken hands with, I asked him, "So, how do you know Q-Tip [rapper from A Tribe Called Quest]?" and LeAlan said, "I don't."

I recognized the gesture between these two young black men in America as generous and elegant, open and inspiring. These, I thought, in their easily pronounced and actual recognition of each other as black men in the struggle of collective character, are the kind of men who could be trusted to perform the delicate "social surgery" that Du Bois recommended for this country one hundred years ago—the critical procedure that will allow this society to see us as individual human beings.

LeAlan Jones

ironically, I was a guest on the radio show "Democracy Now" during the same broadcast as David Levering Lewis, the man who won the Pulitzer Prize for his biography of W. E. B. Du Bois. I was on the program to present an essay I had written about the war in Iraq and the democratization of that region in its aftermath. I wasn't learning about Du Bois for the first time through Lewis, but it was interesting to hear what he was saying about him, even if his presentation seemed a little dry.

I've never read *The Souls of Black Folk*, no. I mean,

since that program segment, I've read a few pages of the book, but I have not read it from start to finish. I live right next to the Center for Inner City Studies in Chicago, so I've definitely heard of W. E. B. Du Bois—that he was one of the forefathers of the civil rights movement in the early part of the twentieth century, that he lectured worldwide, and, of course, that he had an argument with Booker T. Washington. In terms of the quote about healing from *The Souls of Black Folk*, though, I think the healing he hoped for or suggested then is definitely happening today. Just look at hip-hop and what's going on with Def Jam poetry, and the vast array of people who use the spoken word to talk about their own personal issues and experiences.

Eminem, for example, is respected by African American people for his struggles, and we can identify with him, because we can see when it's real, when it's not falsified or manufactured. Sure, he's marketed, but he comes from Detroit. Detroit hasn't been right since the riots—no economic infrastructure at all—so for anybody to come through there and succeed is something to respect. Eminem faces the same sorts of struggles that a lot of black rappers face, and so part of the healing is about having respect for those shared hardships—having problems with your baby mother, your girl. The world expected Eminem to end up some kid in Detroit selling burgers, bussing tables, or working at the factory. He said no to that. He said, "I'm going to be creative with rhymes," and by doing that, he has introduced rap, a black form of communicating, to a white-trash, trailer park mentality. We gave this black form of art and poetry to him, and he has used it as a coping mechanism. That's a beautiful thing.

What separates Eminem from, say, that whole Wigger movement of a decade or so back is that he has evolved through it—like the kid in Atlanta who starts out believing in the Confederate flag but then ends up wearing a Michael Vick [a black NFL quarterback for the Atlanta Falcons] jersey. Kids don't start out knowing the difference between black and white. It's when they get older and start to explore out of curiosity and human nature. It's the white girl who wants to take the black basketball player to the prom at an integrated school, and somebody has to tell her that there will be recriminations because of that action. And then she has to make a choice.

When I was a kid, I would hear the words *white* and *black* being used, and the difference between those two words became clear to me when I started to think about what my goals were and what I wanted to excel at. White people had the nice house, their own space—you know, *Family Ties*, *Night Court*, *Dynasty*—white people always seemed to do things a little bit better, to have more influence. Then, when *Cosby* came on, I realized that I could be Theo and go to college, or grow up and marry Rudy. And even though there was just the one show with black people having a nice life and nice things, I understood that these images of wealth and success, both black and white, were circumstances being dictated by aptitude. A white kid from a trailer park in Appalachia is about as likely to make it as a black kid from the projects on the South Side of Chicago. And that's what makes Eminem as valuable as, say, 50 Cent, because Eminem has shown us the cracks in white culture that have been hidden for so long. We're all accustomed to seeing the cracks in black culture, and now we can see that every white cat can't be living large if Eminem came up out of what and where he did.

Of course, with all due respect to Eminem, no one is denying that he's white, and that there are certain ways and things about black people that cannot be imitated. Swagger, for one thing, and eternal optimism, for another, because what else is there? We started out as a people who were told that we couldn't make classical music; we couldn't speak this way or that, or learn certain skills. So what we did was to get the instrument, the device, or the skill, and then add our own thing to it—figure out the science of it later. And I think what we're seeing now is a younger generation of the Talented Tenth that Du Bois wrote about, a generation that is not only figuring out the science but inventing the science.

People who have suffered have a wisdom that no one else has, and a way of applying that wisdom to their everyday lives. Oprah—from Tennessee, the country—who loves her? White women who want the perfect look, the perfect lives. It doesn't matter whether or not she's respected by those white women. I don't care how she did it or who respects her—she can connect with mainstream culture in a way that no one else can. Like I said, we'll figure it out later. All I know is that we got it. We didn't come here to smoke crack.

My sense of Du Bois as a man—and not to sound disrespectful—is that he was almost like a pimp of his time, because pimps are effective; they get the point across as smoothly as possible, while at the same time making you feel good about yourself and making you look at yourself. With *The Souls of Black Folk*, Du Bois wrote a timely book that reached the right people. He couldn't be too radical back then—like, you know, To hell with you all. We gonna get the hell up outta here. Begin to get your things together so that we can *go*. Let's break. No, Du Bois said, Look, we're really trying to be here, and I don't know what being here is, exactly, but I've seen what's behind us, so let's try another way.

Sooner or later, people are going to have to see beyond the color line into a gray world. Gray might not sound too hopeful, but we know what the black-and-white world has given us. We don't know what the gray world will give us. What's hopeful is to wish for something and then to find out what it is. We know that slavery and racism ain't cool. So we're willing to try something else.

Epilogue

In the winter of 2002, I heard, for the first time in my thirty-three years of being my mother's daughter, the story about how she was fired from her job as a salesgirl at a Boston bridal shop because she rented to a black customer. My father mentioned it to me while he was stacking wood or some such thing during one of my annual autumn visits home, and I had no idea what he was talking about. "Oh, didn't she ever tell you about that?" No, she had never told me about that, I replied. "Well, I'll let her tell you, then. Ask her about it." That night during our ritual cocktail hour in front of a bright, serene fire in the living room, I asked her about it.

"Oh, yeah," she said, the cubes in her vodka and grapefruit juice clinking faintly against the glass and glaze of the fire.

"I can't believe you never told me this story. Why didn't you ever tell me this story?"

"I guess I thought I had," my mom said ingenuously, taking a sip of her drink.

"Please, tell me the story."

It was shortly after my parents had gotten married, she said. My mother was pregnant with my older brother, and my father was finishing a joint MFA at Tufts and the Museum School. They lived in a small apartment by the Fens in Boston.

In her words: "I was barely pregnant with Sean at the time I took the job at a prestigious bridal shop in Boston. Every couple of days we were given salesmanship lessons by the manager, who told us that the mother buys the dress, so to concentrate on her. Besides wedding dresses, the shop rented beautiful fancy cocktail dresses. I was told by one of the staff not to rent these party dresses to blacks, 'Negroes' then, because they ruined them.

"A black woman came into the shop one day, and as I filled out the paperwork for the rental, a coworker pulled me into the back room and hissed at me, 'You know that's not our policy!' I said, 'Well, it's not *my* policy.' And I went back out and rented the gown.

"A week later, I was let go—fired, ostensibly, for daydreaming and reading when there were no customers in the store. But I knew that it was because of the incident with the black woman. I was very upset and came home and told your father. I had wanted to tell the people at the shop that I knew the true reason why they'd let me go, but I was too emotional to be effective. Your father took up the banner for me and went down there, insisted on seeing the manager, and told them all what he and I thought of their policies and outrageous prejudice. It was a great vindication for me, and I was grateful for your father's ability to clearly articulate the situation, and to do what I couldn't do at the time."

My mother spoke this story into the orange-rose flames of the fire, sitting in the creaky, dark warmth of the eighteenth-century Colonial house where I grew up. It did not appear that the bridal shop incident had necessarily made her more or less attuned to black culture or the horror of racism. Neither did it seem to confirm any long-held suspicions or politics she might have held. At the time, she had not even given birth to her first child, let alone had any notion whatsoever that she would end up adopting a black child as her third. In her retelling of it, the incident sounded certainly like an unfortunate experience, but one that otherwise merely reflected how badly people could behave, and how universally limited they could be. And she had never made it a point to tell me. Not even in an effort to counter the many attacks I launched her way as an adolescent.

When I was a teenager, especially after I'd returned from a visit with my birth mother, I would often shout at my mother in angry outbursts of judgment and dissatisfaction, complaining about her not being strong enough, strict enough, independent enough, interested enough, financially secure enough, and, worst of all, for being so selfish as not to have given any serious thought to how hard it might be for a black child to grow up in rural New Hampshire. "We thought the world was changing," she used to say with a sadness too deep for tears. And I'd retort, "Yeah, well, ever hear of Martin Luther King, Jr.? He thought the world was changing, too. Look where that got *him*!" We would go around and around—I expressing my vitriolic need to hold her accountable and she offering bruised, yielding explanations—until finally I would turn my back and stomp off in a huff, leaving my mother feeling frustrated and hurt.

She never begrudged me that horrendous behavior, and it pains me deeply to think back on those arguments now, because my mother really did think the world was changing. And maybe it was. But it wasn't her responsibility to see that it did. My mother's responsibility was to love me, to love all of her children equally, and to create and nurture her family in a way that felt best to her. She fulfilled that responsibility. She also always encouraged me to express myself, to believe in myself, and to value my freedom. And when I was a very young child and she couldn't find any brown dolls at the store, she sewed a beautiful doll for me out of soft coffee-colored cloth, with black braided thread for hair. I named that doll Esmerelda, and I still have her. She lives with my parents and is always there waiting for me when I go home to visit. She sits patiently atop the familiar worn comforter on my bed—well loved, brave, brown, and on her own.

I dedicated my third book, *Sugar in the Raw*, a collection of interviews with young black girls in America (1997), to my father, who "introduced me to journal writing and bade me never to forsake it," and to my mother, who "raised a black girlchild in America on sheer conviction and fierce motherlove." My birth mother's response to that inscription was, "I think we both wish that were true." My mother's relatively benign style of parenting, one that she would firmly argue was not benign at all but, rather, "active in peace and love," never rated very high with my birth mother, who, conversely, always demonstrated what love she had for me primarily through a guerilla-style authority and control. Ironically, she often behaved much in the way of the stereotypically perceived black mother who will snake her neck to the left and right, point her finger, and tell you what's what, and who won't hesitate to march her ass down to the school if someone messes with her child—"Don't *make* me go down there!"

It's impossible for me to imagine what my life would have been like had I been raised by my mother alone, without the influence of my birth mother, or kept and raised by my birth mother without the influence of my mother. But in terms of my racial identity, and my very personal sense of black consciousness, I think that in many ways they may both have struggled as much as I did. Today, my mom would say that my blackness was and is secondary to the unique individual she raised and loves; my birth mother would probably maintain that I am, as I have always been to her mind, culturally white and cosmetically black.

Throughout my life, nobody has been able to affirm my blackness as I have for myself, and what that blackness means to me has taken shape through the voices, anecdotes, and experiences you have just read in this book.

List of Contributors

Elizabeth Alexander is a poet, playwright, and essayist, and an associate professor of African American studies at Yale University. Her first collection of poems, *The Venus Hottentot*, published in 1990, features poems that explore the lives of historical black figures. Her poetry, fiction, and critical writing have been widely published, and she has been awarded an NEA artist grant and a fellowship from the Guggenheim Foundation, among other awards and honors. Her books of poetry include *Body of Life* and *Antebellum Dream Book*, and her book of essays, *The Black Interior*, has just been released from Graywolf Press.

Derrick Bell is a leading scholar, social thinker, and a professor of law at New York University. His career began in the Department of Justice, after which he became a civil rights administrator and eventually a tenured law professor at Harvard University. He has written several books, including the best-selling *Faces from the Bottom of the Well* and the recently published *Ethical Ambition*.

Terence Blanchard is a Sony recording artist who was voted Artist of the Year by *Down Beat* magazine in 2000. He has received three Grammy nominations, two Emmy nominations, and has won the Grand Prix du Disque for his album *New York Second Line*. He is also an established film composer and has composed sound tracks for numerous major releases, including *Malcolm X, Eve's Bayou*, and *25th Hour*, which earned him an Emmy nomination.

Julian Bond was a founder of the Student Nonviolent Coordinating Committee (SNCC) and the founding president of the Southern Poverty Law Center. A longtime member of the NAACP board, he was elected chair in 1998. He narrated the critically acclaimed 1987 and 1990 PBS series *Eyes on the Prize*, and the 1994 Academy Award–winning documentary *A Time for Justice*. Bond is a distinguished scholar in residence at American University and a member of the faculty in the Department of History at the University of Virginia. He has taught at the University of Pennsylvania, Drexel University, Harvard University, and Williams College. He is the author of *A Time to Speak, A Time to Act*.

Cory Booker served four years on the Newark City Council before giving up his seat in 2002 to run a controversial race for mayor, which ended with him being defeated by incumbent Sharpe James. Booker is a Rhodes scholar and has earned degrees from Stanford University and Yale University Law School. He is currently the director of Newark Now, a grassroots non-profit organization, and is also a partner at a law firm in Newark.

A'Lelia Bundles is director of talent development for ABC News in Washington, D.C., and New York. She is the author of *On Her Own Ground: The Life and Times of Madam C. J. Walker*, a 2002 Borders Books–Hurston/Wright Legacy Award finalist, a 2001 *New York Times* Notable Book, the 2001 Letitia Woods Brown Book Prize winner (Association of Black Women Historians), and a 2002 Honor Book (Black Caucus of the American Library Association).

Kathleen Cleaver was a major voice in the black liberation movements of the 1960s and 1970s, active in the Student Nonviolent Coordinating Committee (SNCC). From 1967 to 1971, she was the communications secretary of the Black Panther party as well as the first woman member of its Central Committee. After sharing years of exile with her former husband, Eldridge Cleaver, she returned to the United States in 1975. Since graduating from Yale Law School in 1987, Cleaver has combined legal work, teaching, and activism. She has taught at numerous colleges and universities, including Emory College, Yale University, and Sarah Lawrence College. She has been active in the campaigns to free death-row prisoner Mumia Abu-Jamal and former Panther Geronimo Pratt (released in 1997). Her writings and essays have appeared in numerous magazines, books, and newspapers and she is the author of *Memories of Love and War,* a memoir.

Stanley Crouch writes for *The New Republic,* the *New York Daily News,* and several other magazines and newspapers. His collections of essays include *Notes of a Hanging Judge, Always in Pursuit,* and *The All-American Skin Game,* which was nominated for a National Book Critics Circle Award. He is also the author of a novel, *Don't the Moon Look Lonesome.*

David Graham Du Bois is the stepson of W. E. B. Du Bois, and the president of the W. E. B. Du Bois Foundation. A journalist, activist, and teacher, Du Bois spent eleven years in Egypt as news editor of the *Egyptian Gazette* and editor at the Cairo-based Middle East Features Agency. In the 1970s, he taught at the University of California, Berkeley, and served as editor in chief of the Black Panther weekly newspaper. He recently retired as a professor of journalism and African American studies at the University of Massachusetts in Amherst and is at work on a memoir.

The Reverend James Forbes has served as senior minister of Riverside Church in New York City since 1989. He is an ordained minister in the American Baptist Churches and Original United Holy Church of America. His academic degrees include a master of divinity from Union Theological Seminary and doctor of ministry from Colgate-Rochester Divinity School. He has served on the faculty at Union Theological Seminary and currently is a member of the core teaching staff at Auburn Theological Seminary. His honors include being named by *Newsweek* in 1996 as one of the twelve "most effective preachers" in the English-speaking world, being recognized by *Ebony* magazine in 1984 and 1993 as one of America's greatest black preachers, being the recipient of the Alumni Charter Day Award for Distinguished Post-Graduate Achievement in Ministry by Howard University.

Thelma Golden is the deputy director for exhibitions and programs at the Studio Museum in Harlem. Before her appointment at the Studio Museum, she was the special projects curator for Peter and Eileen Norton, contemporary art collectors and philanthropists, who are based in Los Angeles, California. Golden began her career as a curator at the Whitney Museum of American Art in New York City, where she organized many exhibitions, including "Black Male: Representations of Masculinity in Contemporary Art."

LeAlan Jones is the coauthor with Lloyd Newman of *Our America: Life and Death on the South Side of Chicago*; the book was made into a movie, which was released on the Showtime Network in 2002. He and Newman are among the youngest winners of the George Foster Peabody Award for journalistic excellence and the first African Americans to win the Prix Italia in the last fifty-nine years. Jones and Newman also produced the radio documentary pieces "Ghetto Life 101" and "Remorse: The 14 Stories of Eric Morse," which both aired on National Public Radio in 1993 and 1996, respectively, and which received a Robert F. Kennedy Grand Prize Award.

Vernon E. Jordan, Jr., is one of the major civil rights figures in American history, and he has served as the Georgia field secretary for the National Association for the Advancement of Colored People (NAACP), director of the Voter Education Project for the Southern Regional Council, head of the United Negro College Fund, delegate to President Lyndon B. Johnson's White House Conference on Civil Rights, president and CEO of the National Urban League. He is the author of a memoir, *Vernon Can Read!* He is currently a senior managing editor at the investment firm Lazard Frères & Co., and acts as counsel to the law firm Akin, Gump, Strauss, Hauer & Feld.

Clarence Major is the author of *Configurations: New & Selected Poems 1958–1998*, which was nominated for a 1999 National Book Award, as well as several other books, including *Afterthoughts: Essays and Criticism* and *All-Night Visitors*, a novel. Major has contributed to the *New York Times*, the *Los Angeles Times Book World*, *American Vision*, *Essence*, *Ploughshares*, and *The Kenyon Review*, as well as to over a hundred other periodicals and anthologies in the United States, Europe, South America, and Africa. He has served as a judge for the Pen/Faulkner Awards and the National Book Awards. He has held professorships at Temple University, SUNY-Binghamton, University of Colorado, University of Washington, Howard University, Sarah Lawrence College, and Brooklyn College. He is currently a professor of English at the University of California, Davis.

Jewell Jackson McCabe is a longtime civil rights activist and a businesswoman who serves as director on a variety of boards. She is a presidential, gubernatorial, and mayoral appointee; a consultant to major corporations and cultural and civic institutions; and founder and chair of the National Coalition of 100 Black Women (NCBW), a national women's advocacy organization. As president of Jewell Jackson McCabe Associates, a management consulting firm specializing in strategic communications, McCabe has advised a wide range of corporations in the private and public sectors, including American Express, Matsushita Electric Corporation of America (Panasonic), Reliance Group Holdings, International Business Machines Corporation (IBM), NAACP Legal Defense and Educational Fund, the Metropolitan Museum of Art, and the Solomon R. Guggenheim Museum.

Patricia Smith is a poet, performance artist, and journalist. Her volumes of poetry include *Close to Death, Life According to Motown*, and *Big Towns, Big Talk*, which won the Carl Sandburg Literary Award. She is the coauthor of the nonfiction work *Africans in America*, a companion volume to the 1998 PBS series of the same name, and is currently at work on a biography of Harriet Tubman. Her poems have been anthologized in *Unsettling America: An Anthology of Contemporary Multicultural Poetry* and *Aloud: Voices from the Nuyorican Poets Café*. A four-time individual champion of the National Poetry Slam, Smith has performed her work around the world. She has also written and performed two one-woman plays, one of which was produced by Derek Walcott's Trinidad Theater Workshop. Smith is a former "Metro" columnist for the *Boston Globe* and has been a columnist for *Ms.* magazine and the on-line magazine *Afazi*.

Lalita Tademy is a former vice president of Sun Micro-systems. She left the corporate world to immerse herself in tracing her family's genealogy, which resulted in the writing of her first book, *Cane River*, an Oprah Book Club selection and a *New York Times* bestseller.

Touré is a contributing editor at *Rolling Stone*. His fiction has appeared in *The Source*, *Callaloo*, and *Zoetrope: All Story*, where he won the Sam Adams Short Story Contest, and his essays have been published in *The New Yorker*, the *New York Times*, the *New York Times Magazine*, *Essence*, and *Tennis* magazine, as well as in *Best American Essays of 1999* and *Best American Sports Writing 2001*. He is the author of *The Portable Promiseland*, a collection of short stories, and *Soul City*, a novel.